THE SECRET HISTORY
OF ENTERTAINMENT

THE
SECRET
HISTORY OF
ENTERTAINMENT
DAVID
HEPWORTH

FOURTH ESTATE • *London* and *New York*

First published in Great Britain in 2004 by
Fourth Estate
An imprint of HarperCollins*Publishers*
77–85 Fulham Palace Road
London W6 8JB
www.4thestate.com

A catalogue record for this book is available from
the British Library

ISBN 0 00 719011 5

Printed in Great Britain by
Clays Ltd, St Ives plc

To my wife Alyson and our children
Clare, Henry and Imogen

INTRODUCTION

The expression 'anorak' has become the standard
way of describing any individual – generally a male
one – who takes an excessive interest in minutiae.

But why 'anorak'?

In the 1960s, during the heyday of pirate radio in
the UK, devotees of the stations would take pleasure
trips out into the North Sea to photograph the boats
from which they broadcast. These radio fans were
instantly identifiable by the brand new weatherproof
gear they had purchased for their voyage. Hence
'anorak' became the noun to describe anyone with
the kind of chemical imbalance that would lead them
to undertake that kind of expedition for no reason
beyond the satisfaction of their own curiosity. Or,
indeed, to know any of the stories that follow.

The Secret History of Entertainment is a collection
of stories that not a lot of people know, stories that

explain something of how the entertainment business functions and why some huge and familiar things are the way they are. It touches on the strange lives of stars, the exotic language of the business, the unimaginable wealth of the few, and the hard, complicated struggles of the many. It encompasses huge triumph, utter tragedy and some farce. It deals with everything from why there are no laughs in *The Simpsons* to the economics of hiring The Rolling Stones for your birthday party.

It started life as a feature in *Word* magazine in 2003. This in turn grew out of a conversation in the pub. It was the sort of conversation where people who know too much about nothing very important swap entertainment anecdotage to keep each other amused. If there were two people there who hadn't heard the story before, it went in. This book has been put together in the same spirit. If you know it all already, then bully for you. After you with the anorak.

ELTON goes SHOPPING

Every Monday if he's in the UK, or Tuesday if he's in the US, Elton John buys three copies of the major new record releases, one for each of his homes in Atlanta, Windsor and the South of France.

ROCK AND ROLL was INVENTED by a LOOSE LUGGAGE STRAP

On 5 March 1951, while on their way down Highway 61 to a recording session in Memphis, touring R&B band Ike Turner's Kings of Rhythm lost an amplifier off the roof of their Oldsmobile. At the session, producer Sam Phillips attempted to repair the damaged speaker cone with a piece of cardboard. The resulting distorted sound, the musical equivalent of a folded piece of cardboard jammed in bicycle spokes, became the key element of 'Rocket 88', the Jackie Brenston side cut at that session which is now widely regarded as the first rock and roll record.

The accident that befell guitarist Willie Kizar's amplifier on the road to Memphis can be considered the father of every subsequent attempt to electronically manipulate sound in the name of excitement.

☆ ☆ ☆

THE MAN WHO DIED ON A TV CHAT SHOW

Jerome Rodale was a pioneer of the health and fitness movement of the late 1960s. His publishing company, Rodale Press, launched the very successful magazine *Men's Health*. On 5 June 1971 Rodale, who had predicted he was going to live to be a hundred ('unless I'm run down by a sugar-crazed taxi driver'), was recording an appearance on *The Dick Cavett Show* when his chin dropped to his chest and he appeared to be asleep. 'Are we boring you, Mr Rodale?' Cavett enquired with unseemly levity. It transpired that Rodale had died of a heart attack. The show was never broadcast but the incident later inspired an unforgettable Alan Partridge show in which the eighty-four-year-old Lord Morgan of Glossop expires on the Partridge couch.

☆ ☆ ☆

THE MAN WHO WAS MEANT TO BE BOND

Sean Connery established the physical type for James Bond with his appearance in the first Bond film, *Dr No*, in 1962. But Bond's creator Ian Fleming had someone rather different in mind when he first unveiled his character in the 1953 book *Casino Royale*. In the original description of the agent, Vesper Lynd, first in a long line of Bond girls, describes him as 'very good looking' and says 'he reminds me rather of Hoagy Carmichael … there is something cold and ruthless about him'. At the time, Carmichael's career as a composer of such cosy classics as 'Stardust' and 'Georgia On My Mind' was winding down. He was sixty when the first Bond film was made. He did make a few film appearances, as in *To Have And Have Not*, but remained more comfortable straddling the 88s than wielding the Walther PPK. 'There are other things in life besides music,' he once remarked. 'I forget what they are but they're around.'

THE MYSTERY OF 'WHAT'S THE FREQUENCY, KENNETH?'

One evening in 1986, Dan Rather, one of the best-known figures in American network news, was assaulted while walking down Manhattan's Park Avenue by two well-dressed men he had never seen before. One man punched Rather and kicked him in the back while loudly demanding, 'Kenneth, what's the frequency?' The victim took refuge in a nearby office building and the men ran off. Rather's account of this puzzling incident was widely disbelieved, given his flair for self-dramatisation (he once took to signing off bulletins with the word 'courage'), and his alleged assailant's question was adopted in some quarters as slang to denote cluelessness. In 1997 it was concluded that the man who had set upon him was a disturbed individual named William Tager, by then serving a prison sentence for the murder of an NBC stagehand. At the time, this unfortunate individual was under the impression that the media were beaming messages to him and presumably thought such a prominent member of the media as Rather would know the actual frequency. The incident – or possibly Game Theory's 1987 song 'Kenneth, What's The Frequency?' – inspired REM's song of almost the same name on their 1994 album *Monster*. Dan Rather, who is as averse to personal publicity as most news anchors, subsequently appeared with the group on backing vocals when they undertook a *Saturday Night Live* appearance.

ALEC GUINNESS'S STAR WARS PENSION

Throughout his career the venerable actor Sir Alec Guinness remained obsessed with the fear of losing his new-found prosperity and tumbling back to his very humble origins. (He was born Alec Cuff, the product of a brief liaison between a barmaid and an unidentified toff. 'My mother's a whore,' Guinness once said. 'She slept with the entire crew on Lord Moyne's yacht at the Cowes Regatta.') Even when firmly established as one of the greatest cinema actors of his generation and constantly in demand for work, guests at his Sussex home were horrified at how parsimonious Guinness could be in everyday matters like food and central heating.

In 1975 Guinness had a meeting with an unknown director called George Lucas who wanted him to play Obi-Wan Kenobi in a film he was planning called *Star Wars*. The initial offer made to him was a fee of $150,000 plus two per cent of the producer's profit. This was the kind of generosity they needed to show to get a respectable name like Guinness to put on the marquee. The favourable critical reaction to the film's release cheered him considerably, though he had no inkling of what a monster he had helped spawn: 'This could bring me in $100,000 if it does *Jaws* business as predicted.'

Unprompted and encouraged by the early box-office returns, George Lucas then asked him to take another quarter per cent, and Guinness's diaries record his satisfaction at this 'temporary fortune'. 'The bank telephoned to say they'd received £308,552,' he wrote on 1 February 1978. More money followed, but the publicity attending the movie's success attracted the Inland Revenue, who subsequently made life hard for Guinness. For the rest of his life he was indignant about claims made in the press about his *Star Wars* earnings. Even though he found the films irritating and the experience of making them dull, he signed up to do cameos in the next two movies and cheques kept appearing throughout the early 1980s. In November 1983 he greeted one for

$250,000 with rare delight: 'That will pay for our daughter's schooling, our Italian holiday and our pre-filming holiday in India.' His co-star Harrison Ford, who was one of the few members of the *Star Wars* cast with whom he struck up a rapport, used to refer to him as 'The Mother Superior' behind his back.

KENNETH WILLIAMS'S LAVATORY

A walking parody of fastidiousness, the late *Carry On* actor and radio performer was neurotically suspicious of human society and utterly obsessed with hygiene. He lived alone in a flat in the West End of London where he kept clingfilm over his cooker to ward off germs. He never invited his friends round for dinner because, he said, 'I can't stand the idea of another bottom on my loo.' On the rare occasions that people did drop in on him unexpectedly they were asked to use the facilities at the hotel across the road from his flat.

DAVID BOWIE'S EYES ARE DIFFERENT COLOURS

When the young David Jones of Bromley was thirteen he was involved in a fight over a girl with a school friend called George Underwood. This resulted in his taking a blow to his left eye from a fist (and not a pair of compasses or a toy airplane propellor as some more lurid accounts have it), which caused him to be hospitalised for over four months. At first he was in danger of losing his sight altogether, but ultimately he was left with a permanently enlarged pupil in his left eye. This still shows predominantly hazel, in contrast with the natural blue of his right eye. (The rim around the iris is still blue in certain photographs, although the issue may be clouded by Bowie's occasional use of contact lenses.)

Bowie and Underwood, who subsequently played in bands together, have remained close friends since the incident.

THE VOICE OF GOD

If you've ever sat in a cinema and felt the speakers shaken by a voice like a gravel and honey cocktail intoning a script which generally begins with the words 'In a world...', then you have probably heard the work of Don LaFontaine, Hollywood's foremost voiceover artist for the last forty years. Starting as a sound editor, LaFontaine lucked into his multi-million dollar profession one day back in the 1960s, when the actor supposed to voice *Gunfighters of Casa Grande* didn't show up for the date and Don was called upon to speak the line 'In a blur of speed their hands flashed down to their holsters and came up spitting fire'. Since then LaFontaine has done more than 4,000 trailers and is known as the 'Voice of God', a role he has actually performed live from behind a curtain at his local church. LaFontaine still works as often as he feels like today, ferried from date to date in a white stretch limousine. A decent job will make him $2,000 and may take as long as half an hour. However, like most voiceover artists, he has the latest state-of-the-art ISDN technology installed in his home and can work without leaving the house.

THE POCKET SUPERSTAR

Alan Ladd, Hollywood superstar of the cowboy era of the 1950s, was remarkably small for an action hero. He had been malnourished as a child and once burned down the family apartment playing with matches. His mother called him 'Tiny', and when an interviewer once asked what he would change about himself he replied, 'Everything'.

Estimates of Ladd's precise stature begin at five foot four, but even the most generous go no higher than five foot six. Love scenes were always a problem. When he appeared with Sophia Loren in the 1957 movie *Boy on a Dolphin* he had to stand on a fruit box for the love scenes. James Mason made it clear that if he was to co-star with Ladd in the film *Botany Bay* he was not going to do what many of Ladd's male co-stars had done, which was to stand in a trench to save the lead's dignity. Ladd died in 1964, apparently after an accidental overdose of pills and alcohol.

Even at five foot six he was still an inch taller than Dustin Hoffman and the same height as Al Pacino, and would have fitted in with many of the biggest names in Hollywood today. Tom Cruise's official height is five foot seven, while even Tobey Maguire and Joaquin Phoenix claim no more than five foot eight. Michael Caine, who's six foot two, has been around long enough to note the change with what he calls 'the emergence' of 'a generation of very talented small people. Maybe they are more ambitious because they are more angry because they are short.'

THE BABYSITTER WHO INVENTED COUNTRY ROCK

In 1972 Emmylou Harris was a twenty-four-year-old single mother singing folk songs by night in a Washington club called Clyde's. One night Rick Roberts of The Flying Burrito Brothers happened to hear her perform 'It Wasn't God That Made Honky Tonk Angels'. He was so impressed that he returned the following evening with fellow Burrito Chris Hillman. Two nights later, The Burritos were preparing to play a show fifty miles away when they were joined backstage by former member Gram Parsons. He told Hillman he was planning a new record for which he needed a featured girl singer. Hillman said he had heard a fine singer a couple of nights earlier but couldn't remember her name and didn't have her number.

At that very moment a girl fan who happened to be backstage with the band announced that she was Harris's babysitter and obviously had her number. Introductions were made. Parsons and Harris met and sang together. Harris recorded Parsons's first solo album *G.P.* with him and country rock was born. 'I lucked into this whole thing,' said Harris years later. 'One little millimeter would have made the difference. If my babysitter hadn't been at that Flying Burrito Brothers concert and given Gram my phone number, if Gram hadn't come into my life, who knows what would have become of me?'

MONKEE MOMMA MAKES MILLIONS

Bette Nesmith Graham was a single mother working as a typist in Dallas in the early 1950s when she came up with the idea of a white correction fluid that she initially called Mistake Out. She began manufacturing it herself, at first in her kitchen, using her son Michael and his friends to bottle and sell the product to office supply dealers. She changed the name of the product to Liquid Paper and moved into larger premises in 1968, by which time Michael had become a member of the chart-topping Monkees and made more money in a year than her business had done in the previous ten. She eventually sold her share of the business to Gillette in 1979 for $49 million plus a royalty on every bottle for the rest of the century. Sadly she died the following year at the age of fifty-six, leaving her son with a significant amount of money, an important collection of the work of women artists and a charitable organisation called The Gihon Foundation.

☆ ☆☆ ☆

ENGLISHMEN WERE THE GODFATHERS OF AMERICAN ROOTS MUSIC

Don Law was born in comfortable circumstances in London in 1902. He sang with the London Choral Society. Young enough to escape conscription in the First World War, he packed his bag in 1923 and emigrated to the United States where he sold etchings in New York and ranched sheep in Alabama before becoming first a bookkeeper and then a talent scout for the American Record Corporation in Dallas, Texas. In those days the northern-based companies were looking for interesting performers in the emergent blues and country fields and would set up their recording equipment in southern hotel rooms, where they would make acetates, buying all rights in exchange for a fistful of dollars.

This Englishman was in charge at a session during Thanksgiving week 1936 in the Gunther Hotel in San Antonio, Texas when one young artist came in, sat facing the corner and played his entire repertoire of blues songs. The young artist was Robert Johnson and the songs recorded that day, 'Crossroads', 'Me & The Devil', 'Hellhound On My Trail' and others, announced the blues equivalent of a Miles Davis or Mozart.

Law went on to have one of the most successful A&R careers in country music, working with everyone from Johnny Cash down. But neither he nor his subsequent boss at Columbia, 'Uncle Art' Satherley, made much distinction between blues, hillbilly and other forms of southern music.

Arthur Satherley was born in Bristol in 1889. He emigrated to America in his twenties and found work in a Wisconsin furniture factory that made cabinets for record players. Moving into the record business, which was starting to flourish in the prosperous years following the War, he graduated to spotting and recording talent such as Blind Lemon Jefferson, Alberta Hunter and King Oliver before becoming hugely successful producing Bob Wills and Gene Autry. According to Donald Clarke's book *The Rise*

& *Fall Of Popular Music,* 'Satherley loved American rural music and regarded all of it as country music, whether white or black, but according to the institutionalised racism of the era it had to be divided into "race" and "hillbilly" music.' Both Law and Satherley were inducted into the Country Music Hall of Fame in later years.

WHICH ONE'S PINK?

The name Pink Floyd may nowadays be associated with psychedelia and the pulsing colours of liquid light shows, but it owes its origins to a very different tradition. Floyd founder Roger 'Syd' Barrett put together the names of two completely unconnected and very obscure bluesmen, Pinkney Anderson and Floyd Council, to make a name for his band. The two men, who both laboured in obscurity in the Carolinas and died in the 1970s, never played together and were never featured on an album together, but for the foreseeable future their names remain yoked in the public imagination.

BROWN M&MS AND OTHER ROCK STARS' RIDERS

'There shall be no brown M&Ms in the backstage area, upon pain of forfeiture of the shows with full compensation' was the line that Van Halen had inserted into their agreement with promoters of their live shows in the 1980s. This wasn't there because the band had particular confectionery preferences so much as to provide them with a stick with which to beat promoters who failed to provide more important things like satisfactory access to a venue or adequate power supply.

But since those simple days the supplies and services stipulated in contract 'riders' tell their own story of the increasing cynicism of the music business and the Napoleonic delusions of some of its bigger names. The following examples were culled from

the excellent Smoking Gun website (www.thesmok-
inggun.com) and come from actual contracts.

Luciano Pavarotti's contract stipulates 'there must be
no distinct smells anywhere near the Artist'.

Whitney Houston's need for accommodation
knows no bounds. 'We need all available rooms in
the building,' says her rider.

Christina Aguilera will brook no impediment
between her and her adoring public, which is why she
demands a 'police escort to facilitate band's arrival at
venue' and warns that 'under no circumstances are
vehicles to encounter any delay due to traffic'.

Barry Manilow, uniquely, can call upon his
legions of faithful admirers no matter where he may
be booked, and his contract simply informs the promoter that 'Barry's fan club shows up at 11.00 am to
decorate his dressing room'.

Elton John is clearly no stranger to the 'do you
know who I am?' gambit, which is why the contract
warns darkly that the star 'will not wear his pass once
he has arrived backstage'.

Cher needs a room just for her wigs.

Years touring the heartland gave Johnny Cash an
unrivalled instinct for what works, which is why he

demanded 'an American flag is required in full view of the audience throughout the show'.

There are certain things that not even the biggest show can afford to carry around, which is why Michael Bolton expects the promoter to provide 'the services of the best African/American or ethnic/mixed gospel choir in your market'.

Like a true Brit, Joe Cocker feels that the whole event should be built around drinking. His contract is most specific about the proper temperature: 'Beer to be iced at 6 pm, re-iced at 8pm and again at 10.45 ("With A Little Help From My Friends")'.

Busta Rhymes could just be showing off when he asks for 'one box of Rough Rider condoms (ribbed)', but it's best not to ask.

Foo Fighters are known as a group with a sense of humour and a due sense of their place in the scheme of things. Hence they quietly assert that they 'shall not be required to share a dressing room with any other performer, except Supergrass, Oasis or maybe Led Zeppelin'.

BB King will be on the bus and halfway out of town by the time the crowd have got to their feet to applaud, which is why under 'After-show food and beverages' he ticks the box marked 'nothing'.

Ever since the 1960s James Brown has sought to foster the illusion that his act puts such a strain on him that his health is in danger whenever he is on stage. The promoters are warned: 'There must be an oxygen tank and mask on stage at all times'.

Finally, Chuck Berry never encumbers himself with such frills as a band. He expects the promoter to be ready with 'three musicians including drummer with set of drums, one pianist with piano and one bass player and bass'.

DELIA **SMITH** MADE THE *LET* IT **BLEED** CAKE

Arguably rock and roll's most famous piece of patisserie, the garish cake on the front of The Rolling Stones' *Let It Bleed* album was baked by a young Delia Smith. At the time, August 1969, the album was destined to be called *Automatic Changer* and designer Robert Brownjohn was given a budget of £1,000 to produce the sleeve. Delia Smith, meanwhile, had just begun a column in the *Daily Mirror* and was a jobbing freelance home economist working for a food photographer.

'One day they said they wanted a cake for a Rolling Stones record cover,' she said later. 'It was just another job at the time. They wanted it to be very over the top and as gaudy as I could make it.' The confection, which sat upon a can of film, a tyre and a clock face, is a glacé-cherried paean to gaudiness, making it one she made earlier which has outlived all others.

CHANGING SEX IN SHOW BUSINESS

Changing one's gender is difficult enough in civilian life. In show business it rarely escapes comment entirely. In her biography, the composer and synthesiser pioneer Wendy Carlos makes no mention of the fact that her first records, *Switched On Bach* and the music from the soundtrack of *A Clockwork Orange*, originally came out in the late 1960s under the name of Walter Carlos. She recently successfully took action against the avant-garde group Momus for including a song speculating about the prospect of a marriage between her male and female selves. The Walter Carlos records have since been 're-badged' as Wendy Carlos albums.

Wally Stott was one of the most distinguished arrangers of the 1960s, responsible for the sound of hits for Frankie Vaughan and Shirley Bassey, the soundtrack of *The Looking Glass War* and, probably most famously, the distinctive tuba tune which is forever linked in the memory with *Hancock's Half Hour*. Since the late 1960s his work, including the Academy Award-nominated arrangements for *The Little Prince* and *The Slipper and the Rose*, has been appearing under the name Angela Morley. She now lives and works in Arizona.

Transsexuals working in the punk rock field didn't match the discretion of the two above. Wayne County (born Wayne Smith in 1947) was a member of the Warhol circle and was already performing in drag when he was signed by David Bowie's management in 1973. In the late 1970s he underwent surgery and re-emerged as Jayne County, under which name she continues to perform. Her life and times are chronicled in the book *Man Enough to be a Woman*.

'HAPPY BIRTHDAY' IS STILL IN COPYRIGHT

The song was originally written by the Hill sisters in the United States in 1893. Patty Hill was an educator while Mildred became a musical scholar. They came up with the tune and the original lyric 'Good morning to you', intending it to be used by the pupils as a sung greeting at the beginning of a school day. The song was published in a book under the name 'Good Morning To You'. By 1924 it had re-surfaced in another collection with the words we sing today, and in that form it popped up in a number of Hollywood films, thus increasing its popularity further. A third Hill sister moved to protect the song's copyright in 1935, which should have meant its falling into the public domain in 1991. However, further copyright extension legislation has meant that it remains the property of its publisher until 2030, by which time somebody may have found a way of extending it further.

You are not breaking the law if you sing 'Happy Birthday' to your children without paying, but if you were to launch into it in a crowded restaurant you could be. But, in one of those resounding ironies with which the history of publishing is littered, nobody knows the name of the person who first put the 'happy birthday' words to it and thus provided us with a reason to sing it in the first place.

SOME OF THE BEST LINES ARE MADE UP ON THE SPOT

The script just says: 'Travis looks in the mirror'. The remainder of the 'You talkin' to me?' speech in *Taxi Driver* was improvised by Robert DeNiro.

The line 'My name is Forrest Gump. People call me Forrest Gump' was ad-libbed by Tom Hanks while the cameras were rolling, and kept in by the director.

In *Midnight Cowboy*, the famous scene where Dustin Hoffman is almost run over by a cab and then slaps the bonnet yelling, 'I'm walking here!' was an accident. The cab was not even part of the production.

The kiss in the street at the end of *Lost in Translation* was invented on the spur of the moment by Bill Murray and Scarlett Johansson.

The sudden spit in Robert DeNiro's face in the Russian roulette scene in *The Deer Hunter* was improvised by Christopher Walken with the connivance of director Michael Cimino. It took DeNiro by surprise and thus produced the effect the director wanted.

In *The Mask*, Jim Carrey is being chased by gangsters and pulls a wet condom out of his pocket, saying, 'sorry, wrong pocket'. This was invented by Carrey.

In the famous ear-slicing sequence in *Reservoir Dogs*, the policeman, while pleading for his life, says he has a child at home. Michael Madsen was so thrown he had difficulty completing the scene.

The legendary sex scene between Julie Christie and Donald Sutherland in *Don't Look Now* was improvised on set to give the couple another dimension to their lives.

Near the end of the remake of *Ocean's Eleven*, the conspirators gather around the Bellagio's fountain. They were encouraged to line up and then leave in whatever order seemed natural.

Joe Pesci's 'What, am I funny?' routine in *GoodFellas* was improvised by the actor based on his own experience of dealing with a gangster when he was running an Italian restaurant.

JACK NICHOLSON GREW UP THINKING HIS MOTHER WAS HIS SISTER

In mid-1974 Jack Nicholson was called by a fact-checker for *Time Magazine*, which was preparing a cover story about his upcoming film *Chinatown*. Could he confirm that the woman who had brought him up was not his mother but actually his grandmother? And furthermore, was he aware that June Nicholson was not, as he had thought, his sister but actually his mother? Nicholson was thirty-seven at the time; both his mother and grandmother had died. The news was a profound shock but he was able to have it confirmed by his mother's sister Lorraine.

This was not an uncommon circumstance in the days when children born out of wedlock were the focus of shame. Dancer June Nicholson was seventeen when she got pregnant and it was agreed that she would disappear to New York to have the baby. Her mother would then return from her own apparent 'confinement' with the baby, which would be raised as her own. In fact Nicholson has no birth certificate. Instead there is a Certificate of a Delayed Report of Birth which was issued when he was already seventeen and working as an office boy in Hollywood.

Eric Clapton was nine when he discovered that his 'sister' Pat was actually his mother, and Rose Clapp, the woman he had called mother, was actually his grandmother. Clapton was born in Surrey in 1945, the child of a brief liaison between a sixteen-year-old girl and a Canadian serviceman stationed in Britain. The man, called Edward Fryer, was a semi-professional musician who was given a dishonourable discharge after going absent without leave in England. On returning to Canada he married at least twice and died in 1985, penniless except for a sailing boat.

THE TRAGIC LIFE AND LONG DEATH OF JACKIE WILSON

Next time you hear the distinctive strains of 'Lonely Teardrops' or 'Reet Petite' brightening up the soundtrack of a TV advert, spare a thought for its singer, the great Jackie Wilson. Wilson lived a life which was brutal and incident-packed, even for an R&B singer of the 1960s. Born into a poor family in Michigan, Wilson was drinking regularly by the age of nine and married at seventeen after his girlfriend became pregnant. In detention following petty crime, he learned to box and developed the footwork which would be a hallmark of his stage act.

His singing career took off when he joined the Brunswick label in 1957 (even though his manager died the day he signed the deal). His new manager had mob connections and one story has Wilson being held out of the window of a high-rise building by thugs while his spare hand signed a renewal of his contract. In 1961 one of Wilson's girlfriends shot him after finding him with another of his numerous lovers. His wife was on his arm when he came out of the hospital a month later. The bullet was too near Wilson's spine to be removed and remained there for the rest of his life.

In 1967 he and his drummer were arrested on so-called 'morals charges' in South Carolina after being found in a motel room with two white women. The IRS seized his home over the issue of unpaid taxes; not long after that his wife divorced him. In 1970 his sixteen-year-old son was shot and killed during a confrontation on a neighbour's porch.

On 29 September 1975 Jackie Wilson was performing on stage at the Latin Casino near Cherry Hills in New Jersey when he suffered a massive heart attack. A member of The Coasters, who was first on the scene, got him breathing again and Wilson was taken to hospital where he remained in a coma for three months. He lived on in hospital, semi-comatose, for a further eight-and-a-half years, never saying another word and not knowing how successful his records continued to be. He died on 21 January 1984 at the age of forty-nine.

THERE'S ONLY ONE MANCUNIAN IN FRASIER (AND IT'S NOT DAPHNE MOON)

Jane Leeves was not the only English actor in the sitcom *Frasier*. Sixty-four-year-old John Mahoney, who played Frasier's retired police officer father Martin Crane, was actually born in Blackpool and brought up in Manchester. He moved to the United States as an eighteen year old to live with his war bride sister, completing his education there before working for many years as an editor of medical textbooks. It wasn't until he was in his late thirties that he decided to resume an interest in acting that he'd had as a child. He attended an acting class given by the then-unknown playwright David Mamet. Through his second production he met John Malkovich who invited him to join Chicago's famous Steppenwolf Company.

Mahoney claims to have never been out of work since. He had a small part in one episode of *Cheers* in 1982 and became a regular as the father of Frasier and Niles Crane when *Frasier* began in 1993. Mahoney, who made a conscious decision to lose his English accent in the 1960s, lives in Chicago but plans to retire to England.

KEVIN COSTNER MADE NICK LOWE A MILLIONAIRE

Nick Lowe has worked as a professional musician since 1967. Much of this labour has been in obscurity with bands like Kippington Lodge and Brinsley Schwarz. Despite the odd hit like 'Breaking Glass', he is best known for his production work with Elvis Costello and his doleful sense of humour. It wasn't until 1992 that Nick Lowe found himself called to his one big payday.

This was thanks to a song he had written twenty years earlier called '(What's So Funny 'Bout) Peace Love And Understanding'. Kevin Costner, the star and producer of the movie *The Bodyguard*, was a fan of this particular tune and decided it should be covered by Curtis Stigers and put on the movie's soundtrack. Thanks to the film's success, which hinged on

Whitney Houston's bravura take on the twenty-year-old Dolly Parton song 'I Will Always Love You', Nick Lowe found himself participating in the windfall from the 15 million copies of the soundtrack album that were sold.

He estimates the amount he made to be just under a million dollars, simply for writing that one song, though he cautions, 'It's amazing how not very far that goes.' It enabled him to make a couple more highly regarded solo albums, to tour behind them in not too shabby a fashion and 'to buy a couple of suits'.

MADONNA
CO-WROTE A HIT
WITH A DEAD MAN

Clive Muldoon played in various British rock bands during the 'progressive' era of the early 1970s. With his partner Dave Curtis he formed the duo Curtiss Maldoon who put out an unremarked song called 'Sepheryn'. This had a line that went 'I feel like I've just come home'. Muldoon retired from music and sadly died in 1976.

Twenty years later his niece Christine Leach, a member of dance act Baby Fox, re-worked the song and played it to producer William Orbit. When Orbit got the job of producing the new Madonna album he played it to the star, who added something further of her own and released it as 'Ray of Light' with the following writing credit: Madonna/Orbit/Curtis/Muldoon/Leach. Along with the album of the same name, 'Ray of Light' became one of Madonna's biggest hits. Dave Curtis, who had also retired from music and gone back to college, received over a quarter of a million dollars in royalties in 1999.

HARRISON FORD HAS THE RUNS

In 1981's *Raiders of the Lost Ark*, Harrison Ford is being chased through the casbah by a succession of increasingly threatening characters. He ends up confronting a huge Arab warrior who is wielding a scimitar above his head in a blood-curdling fashion. The original idea was that Ford would defeat the man in a bullwhip-versus-scimitar fight that would have taken three days to shoot. The temperature in Tunisia at the time was 130 degrees and Ford had been suffering from dysentery. The actor persuaded director Steven Spielberg to resolve the fight more quickly, suggesting, 'Why don't I just shoot the son of a bitch?' They tried it with Ford looking at the man and then unexpectedly – with a look of infinite weariness – pulling a gun and shooting him. It still gets the biggest laugh in the film.

☆ ☆ ☆

BRUNO BROOKES, BOB HARRIS AND 35,000 RECORDS

When veteran radio and TV presenter Bob Harris married for the third time in 1991, he and his wife Trudie bought a flat in Hampstead from fellow Radio One DJ Bruno Brookes. Because they could not raise the full purchase price it was agreed that Brookes would furnish them with a two-year interest-free loan of £130,000. It was intended that this could be repaid out of Harris's earnings or through the re-sale of the flat.

The problem was that the next year saw Bob Harris lose his regular slot on Radio One in a wholesale facelift of the station's schedules. At the same time the housing market took a marked dive. He found that his income had largely evaporated and his property was worth significantly less than it had been. Brookes, however, wanted his money and served a repossession order. Harris and his wife moved to a rented property in Oxfordshire where they were woken early one morning by bailiffs with orders to seize the DJ's collection of 35,000 records and CDs. These were to be impounded by the court and sold to pay Brookes what he was owed.

The ensuing court case turned on an argument that goes to the heart of the changing shape of radio, particularly in a computerised age, reflects the differing world views of daytime and night-time radio and pierces the patina of mateyness which broadcasting organisations present to the world. Harris's contention was that the records were as much 'the tools of his trade' as a bricklayer's trowel; to impound them would be to rob him of his livelihood. He gave evidence, in which he was supported by many from the hippier end of the industry, that his shows were 'built' at home and subsequently taken into the studio for broadcast.

Brookes, on the other hand, countered that he had been a top DJ for many years and as far as he was concerned programmes were put together by producers. The presenter, who essentially came in and talked in the gaps between the tunes while reading from a running order, had no need of such a large record collection. Anything he needed to play could be ordered from the record library.

Harris won the case. Brookes lost again on appeal and had costs awarded against him. In 1995 he instigated bankruptcy orders against both Harris and his wife. In recent years Harris, who described the period of the court case as the worst of his life, has been restored to national prominence on Radio Two. Brookes runs a company which programs in-store radio for retailers like Dixons and Lloyds Pharmacies.

FARGO IS NOT A TRUE STORY – BUT THIS IS

The 1996 Coen Brothers movie *Fargo* begins with the caption: 'This is a true story. The events depicted in this film took place in Minnesota in 1987.' It isn't and they didn't.

When a twenty-eight-year-old Tokyo woman called Takako Konishi turned up in Bismarck, the capital of North Dakota, in November 2001, speaking no English and carrying a rough map on which she had drawn a road and a tree, she seemed to be saying the word 'Fargo'. The police came to the conclusion that she had come looking for the ransom money buried and never recovered by the bungling gang in the movie. They tried to explain to her that despite the opening titles, *Fargo* was entirely fictional.

She apparently didn't take the hint and the

following day they took her to the bus station to catch the Greyhound in the direction of the town of Fargo in the adjoining state of Minnesota. The police next heard of her when they were called by the Minnesota police with sad news. They had found Takako's body out in the woods with a policeman's card among her effects. When her death was linked with the story of the movie the press descended on the area and it ran all over the world as 'Japanese tourist dies looking for *Fargo* money'.

The real story, subsequently uncovered by film-maker Paul Berczeller, was more complex. He found that Takako Konishi was a Tokyo office girl who had suddenly gone off the rails, probably following an affair with an American businessman that had gone awry. She had visited Minnesota three times before, begun drinking heavily and may have worked in the Japanese sex industry. She had sent her parents a suicide note before she had made the last journey to Fargo. She was clearly in search of more than money.

THE ROLLING STONES ACTUALLY HAD SIX MEMBERS

The Rolling Stones first formed in 1962 when Mick Jagger and Keith Richard allied themselves with Brian Jones and Ian Stewart. Stewart played the piano. He also held down a proper job at ICI which meant that he was sometimes called upon to feed the other three, who didn't work and were inclined to stay in bed until the evening. With the addition of Charlie Watts and Bill Wyman, The Rolling Stones first made their name around London as a six-piece.

In the spring of 1963 they signed a management contract with Andrew Oldham who immediately told them they had to drop Stewart from the line-up because his face, literally, didn't fit. A calcium deficiency as a child had left him with a jaw that tended to grow large. Oldham has since said that he encouraged the band to fire Stewart because the public would never be able to accurately remember the names and faces of a six-piece group. Whatever the reason, Stewart was grievously disappointed but eventually adjusted to his new role as road manager and occasional piano player. During the band's early American tours he would sometimes play unseen behind the curtain. In the studio he played on everything from 'Around And Around' to 'It's Only Rock & Roll'. He was with the group at every stage between 1962 and his death. When he died of a heart attack in a doctor's waiting room in 1986 it had a profound effect on the rest of the group. 'He was the band's spine,' says Bill Wyman. 'Stu was the one guy we tried to please,' added Mick Jagger.

THE WORLD'S ONLY CELEBRITY DOG

At the end of the First World War, an American army officer discovered a puppy on a battlefield in northern France. He called it Rin Tin Tin after a talisman favoured by French soldiers. He took the dog back to the United States where he taught it to perform tricks. He became convinced that there was a future for the German shepherd in movies and eventually got him a role in *The Man From Hell's River*. The box-office success of this and a score of other films for Warner Bros, who were about to go out of business when he came along, earned him the name 'the mortgage lifter'.

When the first Academy Awards were introduced in 1929, misunderstandings among the electorate led to Rin Tin Tin winning the vote for Best Actor. The authorities moved smartly to give the award to Emil Jannings, who didn't have the grace to turn up on the night and insisted on collecting his award earlier. The original Rin Tin Tin, who received 10,000 fan letters a week at the height of his fame, died peacefully in 1932, cradled in the lap of sex kitten Jean Harlow.

THE HISTORY OF FUCK AND THE MOVIES

In November 1965, when critic Kenneth Tynan caused a major scandal by asking in the course of a live TV debate what exactly was wrong with the word 'fuck', director Joseph Strick was already planning the first film adaptation of James Joyce's profanity-studded novel *Ulysses*. Released in 1967, it was the first movie featuring the f-word to be granted a certificate by the British Board of Film Classification. Distributors around the world handled this art movie as if it were a highly unstable chemical. In New Zealand it could only be shown in front of single-sex audiences, and it was not actually granted any certificate to be shown in Ireland, Joyce's home-land, until 2000.

Michael Winner's *I'll Never Forget What's'isname*,

which was released in the same year as *Ulysses*, featured the line 'Get out of here, you fucking bastard' issuing from the cupid lips of Marianne Faithfull. Robert Altman's *M*A*S*H*, which came out in 1970, was the first Hollywood release to feature the word (although it wasn't in the original script).

In the 1990s, economic, incisive use of the expletive eventually gave way to scripts in which 'fuck' as verb, noun or any other part of speech was sprayed around as often as the most common preposition. This coincided with a glut of films about unpleasant gangsters impersonated with surprising relish by actors who would run away as fast as the rest of us were they ever to come into contact with the real thing.

There is no absolute measure of which movies have gone in for bulk deployment of the f-word, but it is known that the Robert DeNiro film *Casino* uses it 442 times and that *25th Hour* manages to insert it forty times in one five-minute speech. When Al Pacino's girlfriend in *Scarface* (206 times) asks, 'Can't you stop saying "fuck" all the time?', the casual viewer is forced to concede that she is on to something.

Other, more advertiser-sensitive media have coined their own euphemisms. *The Hitchhiker's Guide to the Galaxy* inventively substitutes the verb 'zark'; the cartoon Judge Dredd goes for 'drokk'; and the TV space fantasy *Red Dwarf* 'smeg'. Most successfully of all, Norman Stanley Fletcher of *Porridge* favoured 'naff', while Father Ted miraculously managed to get away with the one letter change involved in 'feck'. This reached its apogee in the following exchange between two characters:

Mrs Doyle: What would you say to a cup of tea, Father?

Father Jack: Feck off, cup!

☆ ☆ ☆

ICI ON PARLE HIP HOP

Avoid embarrassment in the 'urban' section of your record shop with this guide to tricky pronunciation.

Kelis: Kuh-leese
Wyclef Jean: second name pronounced the French
    way
50 Cent: Fitty Cent
Eric Benet: Beh-nay
Beyoncé: Bee-yon-say
GZA: The Gizza
RZA: The Rizza
Me 'shell Ndegocello: N-day-gay-o-chello
Aaliyah: Ah-lee-ah
Stacie Orrico: O-reeko

RICHARD GERE OWES HIS CAREER TO JOHN TRAVOLTA

When Richard Gere first came on the Hollywood scene in the late 1970s, John Travolta was the pre-eminent male superstar of the day and as such every script of any consequence was offered to him on a silver platter. He turned down *Days of Heaven* (1978) and the part provided Gere with his early break. Two years later, Travolta's agent advised him not to take the title role in *American Gigolo*. That became Richard Gere's big hit picture. Worse was to come. Travolta didn't fancy the role of Zack Mayo, therefore Richard Gere ended up wearing the naval whites in *An Officer and a Gentleman* (1982).

This continues to the present day. When *Chicago* swept the board at the 2003 Oscars, the muffled noise in the background would have been John Travolta kicking himself for turning down the part of Billy Flynn, which had gone to Richard Gere, a man never previously known for his dancing. Travolta graciously congratulated Gere on his success, adding, 'How I would have loved to have showed them all what I can do one more time.'

WORKING
TITLES

The name of a movie may be set in stone from the beginning. *Titanic*, for instance, was never going to be anything else. The producers of *Bridget Jones's Diary* weren't going to spend all that money on the rights to a best-selling book and then call it *A Single Girl* or *Big Knickers*. But many movies try out a number of working titles during development and production, often changing their minds only at the very last minute after discussions with the sales and marketing arms of the studios. It was only when some radio stations threatened not to take ads for a movie called *Sexual Perversity in Chicago* that its name was changed to *About Last Night*.

Kevin Costner's baseball movie was going to be called *Shoeless Joe* after the legendary baseball star referred to in the script, before it was decided to give it the more female-friendly name *Field of Dreams*. The Julia Roberts–Richard Gere hooker picture was known as *$3,000* after the transaction between the two of them, but changing the title to *Pretty Woman* simultaneously changed our perception of the film (and presumably gave the female lead a spring in her stride).

The Full Monty is an expression that has burrowed its way so far into the English language that it's difficult to credit the idea that the movie was once going to be called *Eggs, Beans & Chippendales* in homage to P. G. Wodehouse's comic novel *Eggs, Beans and Crumpets*. Is it conceivable that *Some Like It Hot* would still be regarded as the greatest comedy of all time had it kept its working title *Not Tonight, Josephine* (the latter being Tony Curtis's female character in the film)? The other great drag comedy *Tootsie* was going to be called *Would I Lie To You?*, but was re-christened after Dustin Hoffman's mother's pet name for her son.

Anhedonia is a psychiatric terms for the inability to enjoy pleasure. It was also Woody Allen's preferred name for his 1977 film until mere weeks before its release. In tests, audiences clearly didn't understand the word and expressed a preference for the alternative *Annie Hall*. *Citizen Kane* was *John Q*; *It's a Wonderful Life* was *The Greatest Gift*; *Philadelphia* was *People Like Us* or *At Risk*; The Beatles' *Help!* was *Eight Arms to Hold You*; *Close Encounters* was *Watch the Skies*; while *E.T.* came very near to being called the more prosaic *A Boy's Life*. (The movie theatre in *Back to the Future* claims to be showing both movies.)

One of the great contradictions of the global village is that while street kids in Croatia can make a decent fist of understanding the most arcane American references, the American public has to have everything spelled out for it. Thus when *Bend It Like Beckham* was being released in the United States, some executive seriously proposed changing the name to *Move It Like Mia*. Other counsels thankfully prevailed.

THE **LONESOME** DEATHS OF FRANKIE **HOWERD** AND BENNY **HILL**

Comedian Frankie Howerd died on Friday 19 April 1992. Over the following weekend journalists called around his contemporaries for their tributes. Benny Hill's agent, unable to get hold of his client, passed on a quote expressing how sad Benny was to hear of Howerd's passing. What he didn't know was that Benny Hill was already dead in his flat in Teddington where he would remain undiscovered for some days until neighbours began to complain of the smell.

THE TERRIBLE EARLY LIFE OF RAY CHARLES

'Even compared to other blacks ... we were on the bottom of the ladder looking up at everyone else. Nothing below us except the ground.'

The great soul singer Ray Charles was born in 1930 and grew up in rural Florida. His mother Retha was sixteen and alone. People in their locality were so poor that the local doctor took a large proportion of his fees in farm produce. Ray had a younger brother George to whom he was very close. When Ray was five the two boys were playing around a rain barrel at the back of a local store when George dived under the surface of the water in search of a penny, got into difficulties and panicked. Ray tried to lift him out but couldn't. Despite their best efforts, George died in front of Ray and Retha.

A few months later Ray started to have difficulty opening his eyes in the morning, the first sign of the glaucoma which would take his sight utterly over the next few years. In the absence of a social security system his mother was desperate to know what could be done. She eventually approached the kitchen door of a white family known for acts of altruism in the neighbourhood. There young Ray demonstrated the one gift that his mother hoped might provide him with a living: his burgeoning skill at the piano.

The family advised Retha to apply to have Ray admitted into the Florida School For The Blind, which had a coloured section. The boy was accepted and in September 1937 she put young Ray on the train to make the long journey to St Augustine. He was put in the care of the guard because she couldn't afford to travel herself. His sight was failing; the first train he'd ever travelled on was no more than a dim shape. He was seven years old.

THE AMAZING STORY OF 'BITTER SWEET SYMPHONY'

'Bitter Sweet Symphony' was the key track on The Verve's 1997 album *Urban Hymns*. It was the first tune to carry the band from fringe success to the mainstream after ten years' toiling in the margins. Although penned by the band's Richard Ashcroft, it was admittedly built around a four-note sample of a high violin line from a record made in 1966. Because that line came from a record whose publishing rights were owned by Allen Klein, the fearsome American manager who had handled The Beatles and The Rolling Stones, The Verve's management reached an accommodation with the copyright holders prior to the tune's release as a single. However, when it became one of the biggest selling records of its era the copyright holders decided that it had used more material than had been agreed and took further legal action. This illustrates the profound truth of the old music business maxim: 'where there's a hit there's a writ'.

Richard Ashcroft claims the sample was 'barely audible', but those who've had the opportunity to play the two records together beg to differ. The sample came from a version of 'The Last Time' played by The Andrew Oldham Orchestra (Oldham being The Stones' manager and producer in the 1960s). The legal action that followed the success of 'Bitter Sweet Symphony' ultimately meant that The Verve had to hand over 100 per cent of the song's publishing income to Klein's ABKCO organisation.

But this wasn't your regular story of musician overdoing the 'homage' to another musician and having to pay up as a consequence. These notes had been sampled from a track on *The Rolling Stones' Songbook* on which The Stones' original manager had supervised a bunch of musicians in re-workings of Stones hits. The high violin line had actually been invented by David Sinclair Whitaker, the arranger on the session. Whitaker was working for a fee.

But it doesn't end there. The song Oldham's orchestra were embellishing was 'The Last Time', the Stones hit from 1965, which in turn had a strong similarity to the old Staples Singers song of the same name. If you look on the credits of The Verve's album now you will see that Mick Jagger and Keith Richards are credited as the writers of 'Bitter Sweet Symphony'. Richard Ashcroft gets a nod as lyricist. It is performed by The Andrew Oldham Orchestra. Of The Staples Singers or David Sinclair Whitaker or The Verve there is not a mention. When the song was taken up by Nike for an advertising campaign, The Verve publicly gave their minority share of the $700,000 usage fee to charity, challenging The Stones to do the same. They got no response. The Verve broke up in 1999. The Stones will never break up.

Hoagy Carmichael: this is the way that Ian Fleming thought of his creation James Bond.

Wendy Carlos, the artist formerly known as Walter.

The Rolling Stones with original piano player Ian Stewart (left) who was demoted to roadie.

Rin Tin Tin: he died cradled in the lap of a sex goddess.

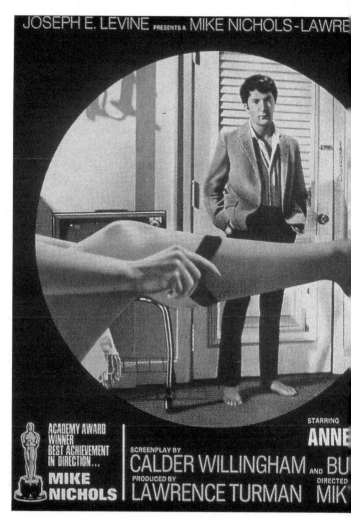

Dustin Hoffman is transfixed by the leg of body double
Linda Gray on the *Graduate* poster.

RMAN PRODUCTION
This is Benjamin
He's a little worried about his future
THE GRADUATE
ROFT AND DUSTIN HOFFMAN · KATHARINE ROSS
SONGS BY
PERFORMED BY
NRY PAUL SIMON SIMON AND GARFUNKEL
OLS TECHNICOLOR® PANAVISION®
United Artists

Oscars rehearsals 2002. Large cutout pictures are placed on the seats which will be occupied by the stars, to enable the camera crews to rehearse their reaction shots.

Patti Boyd inspired George Harrison to write, among others, 'Something'. Eric Clapton wrote 'Layla' about his efforts to win her.

LITERARY
ANCESTORS

The musician Moby, whose full name is Richard
Melville Hall, is the great-great grand nephew of
Herman Melville, the author of *Moby Dick* and
arguably America's greatest novelist. The great-
great-great-great grandfather of Al Murray 'The Pub
Landlord' was William Makepeace Thackeray, the
author of *Vanity Fair*. Daniel Day Lewis is the son of
Poet Laureate Cecil Day Lewis.

I'D KNOW THAT SCREAM ANYWHERE

One specific sound effect has turned up in hundreds of different movies. It was first recorded in 1951 for a Gary Cooper movie called *Distant Drums* and was then filed in the Warner Bros vaults as 'man being eaten by alligator'. There was something distinctive and piercing about this scream which meant that other sound editors were drawn to it. It was used in the 1954 Judy Garland movie *A Star Is Born*, *The Wild Bunch* in 1967 and *The Green Berets* in 1968. In none of these cases did it illustrate the feelings of a man being eaten by an alligator. After it was used in a Western to accompany the sound of an arrow puncturing a character called Wilhelm it became known as The Wilhelm Scream.

The man responsible for making The Wilhelm

Scream part of the contemporary soundscape is George Lucas. His sound designer Ben Burtt reached for it in *Star Wars* to express the surprise of a stormtrooper tumbling into a chasm in the Death Star. It popped up in *Raiders of the Lost Ark* to articulate the dismay of a Nazi as he fell off a speeding truck. Uses in these and other Lucas films have made The Wilhelm into a complex private joke among film-makers. Few films by the likes of Tarantino escape without at least one inclusion. Sound editors play elaborate games to sneak the Wilhelm into movies of all kinds without the director noticing. George Lucas remains as enamoured of the noise as ever. The Wilhelm Scream was used in both of the recent *Star Wars* prequels. It will probably turn up in the last part of the trilogy as much for tidiness' sake as anything else.

THOSE AREN'T JULIA ROBERTS'S LEGS ON THE PRETTY WOMAN POSTER

In fact the only things that are Julia's on the poster that gave hookers their greatest kudos since the days of Christine Keeler are the head and incandescent smile. Everything from the neck down belongs to Shelley Michelle, a model, actress and body double who has also stood in for Barbra Streisand in *Prince Of Tides* and Kim Basinger in *My Stepmother Is an Alien*. 'I wouldn't do nudity in films,' says Roberts. 'To act with my clothes on is a performance. To act with my clothes off is a documentary.'

Shelley Michelle, who was a member of Kid Creole's Coconuts for nine years, fronts a company called Body Doubles And Parts Inc. Body doubles have been blamed by women's groups for the increasingly unrealistic body expectations of young women. It's estimated that 85 per cent of body doubles have breast implants. Despite their hours in the gym and all-salad diets, few actresses are entirely comfortable with the idea of having their bodies projected on to massive screens. Therefore it's become standard practice to use body doubles in nude scenes. Even Kevin Costner's obligatory skinny-dipping scene in *Robin Hood, Prince of Thieves* was done by his body double. Kim Basinger had one throughout *Nine ½ Weeks*. In *Thelma & Louise*, director Ridley Scott assumed that Geena Davies would require a double for her scenes with Brad Pitt. He was surprised to discover that she was happy to do them herself. Being a six-foot-tall former model probably helps one's confidence.

The famous outstretched leg which is hypnotising the young Dustin Hoffman on the posters for the 1967 movie *The Graduate* is not actually that of his co-star Anne Bancroft. It belongs to Linda Gray, subsequently famous as Sue-Ellen of *Dallas*, who has since played the Mrs Robinson role on stage on both sides of the Atlantic.

THEY **KNEW** IT WAS **DIRTY** BUT THEY DIDN'T **KNOW** HOW

Memorably described by critic Dave Marsh as 'three chords and a puff of smoke', 'Louie Louie' is widely regarded as the highest expression of the primal beauty of rock and roll. It was patterned after a local Latin hit and initially jotted down on a napkin by a young LA musician called Richard Berry. His 1956 recording went nowhere and in 1959, needing money to get married, he sold his copyright for $750. That same year his record began to get some play in the Pacific North-west. Over the years various local bands in that region started to make their own covers. One, by The Kingsmen, was considered such a disaster by the group that they resented the fifty-dollar studio fee. It was so sloppily played and recorded that later that year, when it began to pick up airplay in Boston, the rumour somehow spread that the lyrics of 'Louie Louie' were obscene.

There were various interpretations of exactly what made it obscene. The middle verse of one interpretation of the lyric goes 'Tonight at ten I'll lay her again/We'll fuck your girl and by the way/And on that chair I'll lay her there/I felt my bone in her hair'. (Richard Berry has always claimed it was a harmless adaptation of an old sea shanty.) In the light of this furore it was banned altogether by the governor of Indiana, and the FBI responded to parental pressure by launching their own investigation into whether it was undermining public morals. They subpoenaed the master tape and interviewed both Berry and The Kingsmen. After nearly two years and many fruitless hours spent subjecting the tape to rigorous analysis they pronounced it 'unintelligible at any speed' and returned it. The fact that its lasciviousness lay entirely in its sound meant that it escaped the censor.

'Louie Louie' is unique among rock songs in amounting to a small industry in itself. The Kingsmen once did an entire set devoted to just the one song; record companies have released compilations of different versions; it has been proposed as the official song of the state of Washington; radio stations have staged weekend-long 'Louie Louie' marathons; and the 'Louie Louie' parade, in which a bewildering array of musical line-ups from rock bands to barber-shop quartets march down Main Street offering their own particular twist on the famous text, has become a standard charity fundraiser. Richard Berry died in 1997, just two years after a successful action to recover his copyright started to provide him with a substantial income.

NOBODY LAUGHS IN THE SIMPSONS

The Simpsons was the first hit comedy show in American TV history not to have either a studio audience or a 'laugh track'. Hysterical outbursts from the cast aside, there are no laughs to be heard in a *Simpsons* episode, which is very unusual.

Since sound engineer Charles Douglass invented The Laff Box in 1953, the reactions of studio audiences at tapings of sitcoms have been 'sweetened' by the addition of purer, heartier laughs recorded at earlier shows. Some of the laughs we still hear today come from tapings of the Red Skelton and Lucille Ball shows of the 1950s, shows whose sight gags elicited cleaner reactions which are easier to edit. The combination of studio audience and laugh track has produced a form of comedy heavily reliant on regular, climactic wisecracks followed by gales of laughter (see *Friends*).

Because *The Simpsons* doesn't have to wait for the laughter, its writers can layer gag on gag in a way that leaves us caught between gathering giddiness and rapt attention for fear we miss something. A good example is 'The Last Temptation of Homer', where Homer finds himself in a distant hotel room with attractive co-worker Mindy. She huskily proposes the two of them order room service. We immediately cut to Mr Burns's office where Smithers announces, 'Someone is ordering room service on the company, sir!' Burns says, 'Well, we'll just see about that', walks over to a cage of monkeys with wings, opens the door and orders, 'Fly, my pretties, fly!' The monkeys go to the windowsill and plunge to the ground. 'Continue the research,' sighs Burns. This intricate sequence, which lasts less than ten seconds, would be destroyed by a pause for laughter.

There's a further dimension. As *Simpsons* script editor George Meyer puts it, 'With a live audience you always end up with hard-edged lines that the audience know are jokes.' Comedy shows without laughter (*The Office*, *Larry Sanders*, *The Royle Family*, *King of the Hill*) elicit a wider spectrum of responses, encompassing horror, embarrassment, sympathy, rueful recognition and silent smirks on the journey from giggle to guffaw. This is why they win a disproportionate amount of prizes and probably why they tend to remain on minority channels. A laugh track tends to announce the desire to hit the biggest audience possible. Fans of *I'm Alan Partridge* reacted with dismay in 2002 when the series returned with a studio audience. It was the last series.

THE NUDES IN THE DISNEY CARTOONS

In 1999 Disney announced a recall of 3.4 million video copies of their 1977 animation *The Rescuers* after it became apparent that somebody in the background department had inserted two frames of a Playboy centrefold in a window in a scene where two mice heroes fly by. The naked woman would have been on screen for one-eighth of a second, far too brief an interval to be visible to the naked eye.

It was only with the advent of DVD and its freeze-frame technology that the studios suddenly had to stop turning a blind eye to a practice that has been going on ever since the birth of animation. They were terrified that a carefully frozen frame could put them in court for corrupting minors. This had never been a problem in the heyday of animation. Max

Fleischer would allow his animators to insert one frame of Betty Boop naked from the waist up in each of her short films in the 1930s. With these films being projected at sixteen frames per second there was no chance of anyone other than the animators being aware of the gag. Today's animators will still sometimes slip in the odd funny, like a satellite dish among the roofs of a medieval town. The continuance of this tradition has led to growing sensitivity among studio lawyers as rumours have spread via the web that, for instance, the priest in *The Little Mermaid*'s wedding scene had an erection (in actual fact it was his knee), or that the word 'SEX' is spelled out in the sky in *The Lion King* (in fact it spells out the name of the animation studio SFX).

CHOLLY **ATKINS** IS THE **TRUE** FATHER OF **MODERN** POP

Choreography is a key element of the contemporary pop experience. It was not always so. The man who put it there was a former vaudeville tap dancer called Cholly Atkins who was hired by Motown in the early 1960s to organise the on-stage moves of acts like The Temptations and Smokey Robinson & The Miracles.

'He taught us to move in spite of our capabilities,' recalled Martha Reeves of The Vandellas. 'Before he started he would analyse the songs and he would have a mapped-out series of steps for each vocal movement. Our performances had twice the value because of his input.' Atkins took moves from the rich vernacular tradition of African-American dance and added polish from the Broadway musical to provide acts like The Temptations with a sophisticated sexiness that made them naturals for the small screen. The feet planted wide apart and the arms thrust forward pose that begins The Supremes' 'Stop! In The Name of Love' was just one of Cholly Atkins' inventions that have passed into the mass memory. Michael Jackson learned from the same tradition. Everyone learned from Michael Jackson. Atkins died in 2003 at the age of eighty-nine.

ICI ON PARLE HOLLYWOOD

Once upon a time, actors with names like Issur Danielovitch Demsky swapped them for something easier to memorise, like Kirk Douglas. But with renewed pride in ethnic origins and more than a sprinkling of sheer bloody-mindedness, that's no longer the case. Consequently it's never been more important to avoid the hazardous business of launching into the pronunciation of an exotic name without first putting in the spadework.

Milla Jojovich: Meela Yo Yo Vitch
Neve Campbell: It rhymes with 'Trev'
Jake and Maggie Gyllenhaal: Jill-En-Hall
Thandie Newton: Tan-dy Newton
John Cusack: Kyoo-sack

Kim Basinger: Kim Bay-singer

Vincent D'Onofrio: Duh-noff-reeo

Ralph Fiennes: Rafe Fines

Jacqueline Bissett: Beset

Greta Scacchi: Gretter Skakky

Charlize Theron: Charlie's Teron

Rebecca Romijn-Stamos: Romaine

Ryan Phillippe: Fil-uh-pee

Joaquin Phoenix: Waa-keen

Kirsten Dunst: Keersten

Anna Faris: Ahna Faris

Mena Suvari: Meen-a Soo-vah-ri

Heidi Klum: Kloom

Rachel Weisz: Vice

James Caviezel: Ca-veez-ul

Tea Leoni: Tay-uh Leoni

Djimon Hounsou: Ji-mun Hoon-soo

Marton Csokas: Mar-tone Cho-karsh

Franka Potente: Poe-ten-tah

Rhys Ifans: Reese Ee-vans

Ioan Gruffudd: Yo-an Griffith

THE KENNY G-PAT METHENY SPAT

Musicians are notoriously bitchy about each other in private but will very rarely put their feelings on the record. One exception is the normally mild-mannered jazz guitarist Pat Metheny. He was asked by a fan on his website what he felt about the multi-platinum MOR sax man Kenny G's latest album, in which the bubble-headed noodler had taken it upon himself to 'duet' with the late Louis Armstrong via the miracle of digital technology.

Metheny started off by describing Kenny G's music as 'the dumbest on the planet', but that was just warming up for his attack on what he described as the 'musical necrophilia' involved in the duet from beyond the grave: 'When Kenny G decided that it was appropriate for him to defile the music of the man who is probably the greatest jazz musician that has ever lived by spewing his lame-ass, jive, pseudo bluesy, out-of-tune, noodling, wimped out, fucked up playing all over one of the great Louis' tracks (even one of his lesser ones), he did something that I would not have imagined possible. He, in one move, through his unbelievably pretentious and calloused musical decision to embark on this most cynical of musical paths, shit all over the graves of all the musicians past and present who have risked their lives by going out there on the road for years and years, developing their own music inspired by the standards of grace that Louis Armstrong brought to every single note he played over an amazing lifetime as a musician. By disrespecting Louis, his legacy and, by default, everyone who has ever tried to do something positive with improvised music and what it can be, Kenny G has created a new low point in modern culture – something that we all should be totally embarrassed about – and afraid of.'

This, frankly, is the most heartfelt and articulate dis ever publicly delivered by one musician about another. Metheny isn't afraid of the prospect of one day running into Kenny either. 'If I ever do see him anywhere, at any function – he will get a piece of my mind (and maybe a guitar wrapped around his head).' Other musicians rushed to support Metheny in his campaign against the 70-million-selling saxophonist. Guitarist Richard Thompson was moved to compose 'I Agree With Pat Metheny', which goes 'I agree with Pat Metheny/Kenny's talents are too teeny/He deserves the crap he's going to get'.

Fight! Fight!

A **BAD** DAY TO **DIE**

The writers C. S. Lewis (*The Chronicles of Narnia*) and Aldous Huxley (*Brave New World*) both died on the same day – 22 November 1963. Their deaths didn't attract the usual newspaper coverage because John F. Kennedy was assassinated on the same day.

WHY **ELVIS** NEVER **TOURED** OUTSIDE THE **USA**

The biggest star of the twentieth century never toured outside the United States because his manager Colonel Tom Parker didn't want him to. He didn't want him to because he (Parker) had no passport. He had no passport because he had entered the United States illegally. He had entered the United States illegally from Holland (his real name was Andreas Kujik) in the 1930s because, according to some Presley scholars, he was on the run from the Dutch police following the mysterious murder of a woman in his home town. The evidence here is flimsy and circumstantial, but what's unarguable is that the only time Elvis spent outside of the United States was when doing his national service in Germany.

The Colonel would fend off all enquiries about

overseas tours with noises about the inadequacies of security or Elvis's reluctance to play outdoors. In the 1970s he made overtures to Led Zeppelin's manager Peter Grant about the possibility of Grant's overseeing a European tour because 'I will be busy here'. It never happened. Instead he arranged for a broadcast by satellite from the island of Hawaii (the fiftieth state of the Union). When Elvis threatened to take a holiday in Europe, Parker persuaded him against it and instead arranged for him to go to Bermuda. The weather was poor. This seems to have cured Presley of his short-lived wanderlust.

THE LOST WORDS OF STAR TREK

The distinctive theme tune of *Star Trek* was written in the mid-1960s at the time of the original series by Alexander Courage. Courage was a low man on the Hollywood totem pole at the time, which was why he was prepared to put the time into penning a theme for a pilot that might never see the light of day, let alone become a hit. However, when it proved to be a smash he and his descendants were looking forward to the prospect of payments every time it was played. Obviously he couldn't see it stretching ahead for the next forty years, but he saw a windfall none the less.

It was not to be. Courage never got his big payday because *Star Trek* creator Gene Roddenberry pressured him into signing a contract that allowed him to add lyrics to the tune and collect half the royalties.

Roddenberry's lyrics went 'Beyond the rim of the starlight, my love is wandering in star flight' and continued in a similar vein. The words were never recorded and were never used on the programme but that didn't alter the financial deal. Every time the tune was played Roddenberry got 50 per cent.

SORRY, BUT THEY NEVER SAID IT

Captain Kirk never said 'Beam me up, Scotty' in *Star Trek*.

Humphrey Bogart never said 'Play it again, Sam' in *Casablanca*.

The Cary Grant line 'Judy Judy Judy' was invented by a nightclub comedian doing an impression of Grant.

The voice from the sky in *Field of Dreams* did not say 'If you build it, they will come'. Instead it said '… he will come'.

Johnny Weissmuller never said 'Me Tarzan. You Jane' in the Tarzan movies.

James Cagney never said 'You dirty rat'.

Shame.

DYNASTY

The parents of some famous actors:

1. Liv Tyler is the daughter of Bebe Buell, a former model whose boyfriends have included Mick Jagger, Rod Stewart, Elvis Costello, Iggy Pop, David Bowie, Jimmy Page and Steven Tyler. When Liv was born in 1977 she was raised by Bebe and the man she believed to be her father, Todd Rundgren. It was only when she was eleven that she discovered that her father was actually Tyler and changed her name from Rundgren to Tyler. In 2003 Liv married Royston Langdon, a member of the group Spacehog.

2. Gwyneth Paltrow is the daughter of stage actress Blythe Danner, who was nominated for Tony Awards in *A Streetcar Named Desire* and *Betrayal*.

3. Carrie Fisher is the daughter of Debbie Reynolds, who starred in *Singin' in the Rain*.

4. Jamie Lee Curtis is the daughter of Janet Leigh (the heroine of *Psycho*) and Tony Curtis.

5. Melanie Griffith is the daughter of another Hitchcock heroine, Tippi Hedren, who now does wildlife conservation work.

6. Natasha and Joely Richardson are the daughters of Vanessa Redgrave and film director Tony Richardson, and granddaughters of Sir Michael Redgrave and Rachel Kempson.

7. Candice Bergen is the daughter of Edgar Bergen, the ventriloquist whose act with Charlie McCarthy was the most popular radio show in America during the 1930s.

8. Mia Farrow is the daughter of Maureen O'Sullivan, who played Jane opposite Johnny Weissmuller in the Tarzan films.

9. Kate Beckinsale is the daughter of the late Richard Beckinsale (star of *Rising Damp* and *Porridge*) and Judy Loe.

10. Drew Barrymore is the daughter of actor John Drew Barrymore, granddaughter of John Barrymore, and great-granddaughter of silent film actor Maurice Costello.

SHIRLEY MACLAINE AND WARREN BEATTY ARE SISTER AND BROTHER

They are the children of Ira and Kathlyn Beaty of Virginia. Their mother was an actress and drama teacher who encouraged them towards the stage. Shirley dropped the surname and adopted her middle name on arriving in New York at the age of eighteen to be a dancer. By the time she was twenty-one she was already starring in Hitchcock's *The Trouble With Harry*. Her brother followed her to Hollywood in 1961 when he was twenty-four to make *Splendor in the Grass*. They have never appeared in a film together.

☆ ☆ ☆

WHO WAS 'YOU'RE SO VAIN' ABOUT?

In 1972 Carly Simon recorded 'You're So Vain'. Its distinctive refrain was 'You're so vain, you probably think this song is about you'. Because Carly Simon was a handsome, well-connected woman with her share of prominent past lovers, the gossip mills were full of speculation about who could possibly be the subject of her song, a huge hit all over the world. Was it ex-boyfriend Warren Beatty? Was it ex-boyfriend Cat Stevens? Was it ex-boyfriend Kris Kristofferson, by then the companion of Barbra Streisand? Was it possible that the subject was Mick Jagger, and had she further sassed up the gag by getting him to sing backing vocals on it? Or was it her new husband James Taylor, who had indeed flown a jet up to Nova Scotia to see the total eclipse of the sun, as detailed in the song?

The following thirty years have proved one thing: Carly Simon will never be confused with a mug. Whenever the subject came up in an interview she politely declined to identify the individual, while making sure to add a little detail about the candidates. In 2001 she was still being asked and candidly admitted to one interviewer that if she did unveil the culprit then nobody would have anything to ask her about.

Finally, in 2003 she auctioned the identity for charity. A TV producer called Dick Ebersol paid $50,000 for the privilege of taking a few friends for a drink with Carly Simon with the promise that at midnight the name would be vouchsafed to him and only him. The condition was that Ebersol had to sign a confidentiality agreement so the speculation would not end there.

The name of the album that 'You're So Vain' came from is *No Secrets*.

☆ ☆ ☆

HIT MOVIES ARE DECIDED IN THE FIRST WEEKEND

The economics of movie-making are based around the opening weekend. If you don't come out in the top three at the box office over those few days then you will lose screens. If you lose screens you will not be a blockbuster. For instance, when *Spider-Man* opened it took 75 per cent of the money taken at the box office that first weekend. This doesn't leave much revenue for everybody else to fight over.

A great opening weekend can't be guaranteed, but you can insure against failure by hiring a big star. A turkey with Tom Cruise in it stands a better chance than a turkey without Tom Cruise in it. Only twelve actors at any given time can 'open' a film in this way and they demand huge sums for their services. A standard deal might mean that a big name will get a fee of $20,000,000 (plus, say, another five for expenses incurred) against 10 per cent of the gross. This means that as soon as the film has taken $200 million in ticket revenue the actor is then in for 10 per cent of everything else it earns (and some big names even get 15 per cent of every DVD sold). If it flops the star is slightly embarrassed. The star is not embarrassed enough to give the $25,000,000 back, however.

When it goes well the star's earnings boggle the mind. Tom Cruise made $65,000,000 out of *Mission Impossible 2*; Bruce Willis $50,000,000 for *The Sixth Sense*; in signing up for a percentage of the merchandise on *Batman*, Jack Nicholson (who was actually in a supporting role) made money from sequels that he wasn't even in – $50,000,000 at the very least.

The growing problem with this policy of star insurance is that it's become increasingly difficult for studios to make much profit out of single movies. By the time they've paid the star and the big-name director there's not that much to show. Hence the fashion for multi-part films like *Austin Powers* or properties like *The Matrix* with significant ancillary income from games. The second part of *Kill Bill* was announced long before the first part had been savaged by the critics.

In the future we'll probably be seeing more ensemble comedies like *Road Trip*, where none of the actors has the negotiating power to ask for more than scale. What we definitely won't be seeing is the big romantic blockbuster as we might have done in an earlier age. It's no longer possible to have a Julia Roberts playing opposite a Jim Carrey with a Spielberg directing, because by the time they'd all been paid there wouldn't be enough cinemagoers on the planet to carry it into profit. Not even if China comes on stream earlier than anticipated.

BOB DYLAN'S SECRET SECOND WIFE

Bob Dylan loves the ladies. If that wasn't clear from his songs then it's clear from his hectic love life. Even before he was well-known he kept six girlfriends on the go simultaneously at the University of Minnesota. One, Bonnie Beecher, has since nearly been in fights with other women who claim that they were the inspiration behind 'Girl of the North Country'. When Dylan came to New York and became a star, he put his new girlfriend, the seventeen-year-old Suze Rotolo, on the cover of his hit album *Freewheelin'*, but when it fell apart he immediately wrote 'Ballad in Plain D', blaming it all on her sister.

Joan Baez was his first famous partner. For two years they were the Posh and Becks of protest. That was until he ditched her on a tour of Europe, during which he also kept company with model Nico, sixteen-year-old Dana Gillespie, and finally flew in model Sara Lowndes (immortalised in 'Sad Eyed Lady of the Lowlands' and 'Sara'), who was to become his first wife and bear him four children.

Dylan returned to the road in the mid-1970s as his marriage was breaking up and threw himself back into the romantic fray with the same energy. On his thirty-fifth birthday his wife and mother decided to surprise him while he was on tour. They dropped in on him unannounced, finding him with not one but two of his girlfriends. How he talked his way out of that one is not recorded. He clearly has the kind of charm that allows him to, as the saying goes, charm the knickers off the vicar's wife. According to Bette Midler, with whom he worked briefly, 'He absolutely charmed the pants off me – well, not literally, but close. A couple of first bases in the front seat of his Cadillac.'

Dylan continued on his so-called Never Ending tour in the 1980s and began to 'date' his backing singers, who were generally African-American women with strong church backgrounds. In the late 1970s, singer Jo Ann Harris had to be positioned between Helena Springs and Carolyn Dennis on stage because the two were such fierce rivals for the boss's favours. There are some who believe that he actually briefly married Clydie King, one of his singers. This has never been substantiated.

What did emerge recently is that when Carolyn Dennis became pregnant with his child he did the decent thing and married her in secret, even going so far as to briefly set up home with her in the suburban anonymity of the San Fernando Valley. The marriage came to an end in 1992 but Dylan continues to support their child Desiree and it's clear that she will be accorded the same rights to his inheritance as the children by his first marriage.

THE MOST
CONNECTED ACTORS

It started with a parlour game called Six Degrees of Kevin Bacon. Here the objective was to link the ubiquitous Kevin with any other screen actor via the smallest number of mutual projects. The less steps it took, the lower the 'Bacon number'.

A maths professor called Brett Tjaden then calculated the average degree of connectedness of all the quarter of a million actors in the Internet Movie Database. What he found, of course, was that Kevin Bacon, being a relatively young man, was only averagely connected. The truly connected actors were: a) older; b) had stayed in work throughout their careers; c) had done a wide range of work; d) had worked in movies with big casts.

In 2003 the ten most connected actors in the

movies were: Rod Steiger, Christopher Lee, Dennis Hopper, Donald Pleasence, Donald Sutherland, Anthony Quinn, Max Von Sydow, Charlton Heston, Harvey Keitel and Martin Sheen. Lee's Bacon rating had been massively boosted by his appearances in both the *Lord of the Rings* and *Star Wars* series while in his eighties.

THE FACE THAT LAUNCHED A THOUSAND RIFFS

Patti Boyd was an eighteen-year-old model when she got a part as a schoolgirl in The Beatles' *Hard Day's Night*. During breaks in filming George Harrison was signing autographs for fans and putting a kiss at the bottom. When he signed one for her he added seven kisses and asked her out. Within a year they were living together. They were married in 1966.

Patti inspired many of Harrison's greatest love songs, including 'I Need You', 'For You Blue' and, most notably, the song Frank Sinatra called 'one of the greatest love songs of the last fifty years', 'Something'. But by then she was being wooed by Harrison's close friend Eric Clapton. One day Clapton turned up at their house and confronted

Patti with a packet of heroin. 'Either you come away with me or I take this,' he threatened.

Clapton's greatest record, 'Layla', is fired by his unrequited love for Patti. It was based on the Persian tale of Layla and Madjun, which is about a doomed romance with a woman promised to another. (Derek and the Dominoes, the group who recorded it, were a singuarly ill-fated group: guitarist Duane Allman died in a motorcycle accident, bassist Carl Radle died from drug and alcohol abuse, while drummer Jim Gordon, who co-wrote 'Layla', had a mental breakdown and was incarcerated for the murder of his mother.)

By the time Patti left Harrison to become Clapton's wife in the mid-1970s, his drinking had become chronic. One of Clapton's biggest hits of this period, 'Wonderful Tonight', is a sentimental but telling description of what it's like to spend an evening out with a maudlin drunk. 'It's time to go home now and I've got an aching head/So I give her the car keys and she helps me to bed.' Patti divorced Clapton in 1985 and has resisted all offers to write what could be the key memoir of the 1960s and '70s.

HOW TO **MAKE MONEY** WITHOUT HAVING A **HIT**

Many performers will be mourning the passing of the single, because with it goes the little-marked tradition that you make almost as much money from being the performer and writer of a B-side as you do if you wrote and performed the one that everybody is singing and asking for in the shops. (This is one of the reasons why the singles that Phil Spector produced for The Ronettes or The Crystals in the 1960s generally had a tune by The Phil Spector Orchestra on the other side.) If the A-side is a cover, the B-side will generally be one of the songs that the artist wrote himself.

The other, often overlooked source of income is airplay. Every time a song you wrote and recorded is played on national radio or TV you are paid as much as £20 for every minute it's on air. Local stations pay less but there are hundreds of those, and more TV channels all the time. It all mounts up. Even people who haven't had a hit for years can pay their mortgage with their annual cheque from PRS.

THE SIMPSONS
AND THE
GROENINGS

Simpsons creator Matt Groening's mother and father were called Marge and Homer. His sisters were Maggie and Lisa.

WHEN THE **BBC** **CLOSED** FOR **BATHTIME**

In the 1950s BBC television would shut down transmission between the end of children's programmes at six o'clock and the beginning of adult programmes at eight in order to allow the family to have a meal, bathe the children and get them to bed.

DOWN ON HIS LUCK, SINATRA PLAYS BLACKPOOL

In July 1953 Frank Sinatra starred in a week's variety at the Opera House, Blackpool. At the time, his career was becalmed between his success as the bobby-soxer's idol and his Hollywood breakthrough with *From Here to Eternity*, and his marriage to Ava Gardner was on the skids.

Frank Sinatra arrived for a lengthy tour of the Moss Empires with his pianist, Bill Miller, part of which was a week at the Blackpool Opera House. The three main theatres in Blackpool had the same management and their output was piped into an underground room where a technician would listen for faults and go to the appropriate theatre to correct them. A doctor from Leeds asked if he could place a reel-to-reel tape recorder next to the speaker for

Sinatra's show and, against all the odds, he got a near-perfect recording.

On the recording Sinatra praises the fifteen-piece orchestra 'mortgaged and led by the little giant', Billy Ternent. Unprofessionally but entertainingly, Sinatra comments that they are far superior to the orchestra on his last visit, led by 'Wolfie Phillips'. He also blames Mr Lopez, whoever he may be, for the mistakes in the printed programme.

As well as performing thirteen songs during his fifty-minute appearance, Sinatra jokes about the English weather ('I got a parka made in Alaska and had it sent down here'), our passion for tea ('Don't you put anything in it?') and the decline in his career ('They didn't put the hole in the middle of this record'). He parodies Bing Crosby with a spoof lyric called 'Ol' Man Crosby' and also makes jokes about Frankie Laine, Billy Daniels, Perry Como and the British heart-throb Donald Peers. Sinatra is playful throughout the whole performance, announcing that his next record is to be called 'I'm Gonna Put a Bar in the Back of My Car and Drive Myself to Drink', and he says, full of fun, 'Oh, it's a happy night.'

A few months later Sinatra was back in America, topping the charts with 'Young at Heart', winning an

Oscar for *From Here to Eternity*, and divorcing Ava Gardner. Frank Sinatra in Blackpool is a fantastic performance which deserves to be officially released. At one point he says, 'I may set fire to this joint, I don't know.' Maybe the maintenance man was needed after all.

THE OSCARS
REHEARSAL

The Oscars rehearsal takes place the day before the actual show and involves all the star presenters, who dutifully turn up and rehearse their links. In each of the star seats is a life-sized blow-up photograph of the guests, which the cameramen use to practise their reaction shots for maximum smoothness on the night.

AMERICA DOESN'T GET BRITISH COMEDY

Every few years there's talk in the papers of a British comedy hit being taken to the United States. Sometimes it gets as far as a pilot. *Are You Being Served?* was remade as *Beane's of Boston*; *Dad's Army* as *Rear Guard*. In a tiny number of cases these get commissioned. The last example of one becoming a hit was *Sanford & Son* (an adaptation of *Steptoe & Son*) in 1972. The chances of one achieving the same household-name status there as they have here is obscure indeed. Even celebrated and influential shows like *Monty Python*, *Fawlty Towers* and *The Office* never get further than Public Television. This reaches about the same proportion of the population as S4C does here.

The harsh fact is that the great American audience –

no relation to the taste-makers based in New York and Los Angeles – thinks we talk like faggots and doesn't share our sense of humour. The only recent exceptions to this iron rule have been Simon Cowell and Anne Robinson, who have ridden the formats of *Pop Idol* and *The Weakest Link* respectively to success in the United States, largely because no American TV presenters would dream of being as rude as these shows require them to be.

PEOPLE WHO COULDN'T LEARN LINES

Tony Hancock, the TV comedian, found it difficult to learn scripts. In his one-man show *The Bed-Sitting Room* he had lines written on all available surfaces on the set, largely as a back-up. A car crash before the recording of *The Blood Donor* meant that he missed some rehearsals and so the producers allowed him to read most of the script from cue cards. If you watch this classic recording now, it's obvious that he rarely engages the eyes of the other actors and is generally looking over their shoulders in the direction of a cue. Once he'd been allowed to get away with that, he never bothered to learn lines again. On moving to ITV there were times when he wouldn't even turn up to rehearsal, relying on a stand-in to block in the scenes for him.

Marilyn Monroe was never good at learning lines. During the shooting of *Some Like It Hot* it took her no less than fifty takes to nail the elementary line, 'It's me, Sugar'. In one scene she had to search through some drawers while demanding, 'Where's the bourbon?' Because she kept getting the line slightly wrong, Billy Wilder had the correct version pasted inside one – and eventually all – of the drawers.

ROCK STARS WHO SERVED THEIR COUNTRY

Billy Bragg was in a tank regiment of the British army but bought himself out with 'the best spent £175 of my life'. Elvis Presley did his national service in Germany with the 32nd Tank Battalion. Jimi Hendrix had a medical discharge from the 101st Airborne after sustaining an ankle injury in a parachute jump. Michael Nesmith served two years in the US Air Force, as did Marvin Gaye. Terence Trent D'Arby was in the US Army in Germany in the early 1980s and was being considered for the rank of sergeant when he left to become a musician. Jerry Garcia had accrued two court martials and eight AWOL charges when he left the army after a few months in 1960.

THE ALBUMS PREVIOUSLY KNOWN AS ...

The Beatles' *White Album* was going to be called *A Doll's House*, and *Abbey Road* was going to be *Everest*.

Elvis Costello's *Armed Forces* was going to be called *Emotional Fascism*.

The Who's *Tommy* was going to be called *Brain Opera*.

Morrissey's *Viva Hate* was going be called *Education In Reverse*.

Radiohead's *Kid A* was going to be called *ENC* (standing for *Emperor's New Clothes*).

Oasis's *Standing on the Shoulder of Giants* was going to be called *Where Did It All Go Wrong?*.

NOBODY THOUGHT THE WALKMAN WOULD WORK

It is the most commercially successful electronic product ever. Yet when it was born in 1979 few people thought it would catch on. Somebody at Sony in Japan suggested tweaking a Pressman personal cassette recorder (targeted at journalists recording interviews) and adding some headphones to develop something they planned to call the Stereo Walky and then moderated to Walkman in an echo of the Pressman brand.

People within Sony and without had doubts that it would take off for the simple reason that it didn't record. When they launched it in Japan in July 1979 sales were worryingly slow at first. One of the early marketing initiatives was to take it out to parks and allow people to listen to it. When people heard it the effect was like a bush fire. Visiting rock bands like The Police brought the first players back to Europe and America and spread the word. Because it was felt that the word Walkman would never be accepted, the product was re-christened the Sony Stowaway for the UK and the Sony Soundabout for the United States. To date, 200 million have been sold worldwide since its launch.

THE FOUR TOPS' FIFTY-YEAR CAREER

Black American vocal groups tend to be the most enduring acts in music, but nobody can boast the same line-up for as long as The Four Tops. Levi Stubbs, Renaldo Benson, Abdul Fakir and Lawrence Payton started singing together in 1953 and had a string of immortal hits such as 'Reach Out (I'll Be There)' and 'Baby I Need Your Loving' in the 1960s. When Payton died in 1997 they had to make their first change in line-up to bring in Theo Peoples.

MOM IN A BOX

Director Alfred Hitchcock gave the six-year-old Melanie Griffith a doll with an eerie resemblance to her mother, *Marnie* star Tippi Hedren. Because it was packaged in a wooden box, Melanie thought it was supposed to be a coffin.

HOW TO RENT A SUPERSTAR

If you want The Rolling Stones to play your private party, it will cost you more than $5,000,000. In 2002 they performed at the sixtieth birthday of Texan billionaire David Bonderman at the Hard Rock Hotel in Las Vegas. They played for an hour and a half to 500 guests who had come straight from a dinner where they had been entertained by Robin Williams.

Very few performers consider themselves above the private show. Michael Jackson played three concerts for the Sultan of Brunei for a total of fifteen million dollars. Whitney Houston performed at the Sultan's daughter's birthday party. A Californian telecoms millionaire hired Rod Stewart, David Crosby, Journey and Christopher Cross to play his wedding, while a company called Applied Material got Bob

Dylan and his son Jakob's band The Wallflowers to play a show celebrating the firm's thirtieth anniversary.

JUMPING
THE SHARK

Jumping the Shark refers to the point at which a successful TV series outlives its welcome and messes with its basic premise. The expression comes from an episode of *Happy Days* when the previously land-based mammal Fonzie went surfing and avoided a shark by jumping over it. It was coined by Sean Connolly of Michigan in 1985.

Jumping the Shark can occur when a key actor changes (John Boy in *The Waltons*) or when the love interest gets married (Niles and Daphne in *Frasier*). It could be said to have happened with *Friends* when the cast started to get pregnant, or with *Only Fools and Horses* when Del and Rodney suddenly became millionaires. It happened with *Dallas* when Bobby's death turned out to be just a dream. Only a select handful of shows could be said to have never Jumped the Shark. The likes of *Fawlty Towers* and *The Office* guarded against the contingency by stopping after a couple of series. Top of the Never Jumped category on the JTS website is, naturally, *The Simpsons*.

RHYMING SLANG

Aga Saga
Fiction set in the shires. As in: Mary Wesley's *Part of the Furniture*.

Cock Rock
Twelve bar blues married to overt sexual display. As in: The Rolling Stones' 'Honky Tonk Woman'.

Chick Flick
Movie with heavy female appeal. As in: *Love Actually*.

Creature Feature
Horror movie with nasty animal. As in: *Godzilla*.

Creepy Weepie
Sentimental novel with Gothic overtones. As in Virginia Andrews' *Flowers in the Attic*.

Feevee
Pay TV.

Slomo
Slow motion.

Rom Com
Romantic comedy.

Pink Ink
Romantic fiction.

Shock Jock
Provocative radio host.

Teenzine
Magazine aimed at teenagers.

THEY *DIED* WITH *THEIR* SLAP ON

R&B singer Johnny Ace was amusing himself back-stage between shows in 1955 with a game of Russian roulette and accidentally shot himself. In the words of a witness, 'That kinky hair of his shot straight out like porcupine quills'.

Leonard Rossiter missed his cue during a West End performance of *Loot* in 1984 and was found dead in his dressing room.

Sid James actually collapsed on stage during a performance of *The Dating Game* at the Sunderland Empire in 1976 and died shortly afterwards.

Les Harvey, the guitarist of Stone The Crows, died on stage at the Swansea Top Rank in 1972 after being accidentally electrocuted.

Johnny Guitar Watson died on stage at the Blues Café in Yokohama in 1996.

Mark Sandman of the rock band Morphine had a heart attack on stage in Rome in 1999 and died in the ambulance.

Tommy Cooper suffered a fatal heart attack during a live TV show in 1984. The audience thought it was part of the act. He would probably have wanted it that way.

GOT THEM ALT.NEO BREAKBEAT HANDBAG LOUNGECORE BLUES

Writing about music, said Frank Zappa, is like dancing about architecture. What he would have made of this dictionary of musical genres we can only guess.

A

A capella

Unaccompanied vocal group. As in: 'Only You' by The Flying Pickets.

Acid House

Booming American dance music meets repetitive, hallucinatory European synthesisers, sparking rave boom of 1988. As in: 'We Call It Acieed' by D-Mob.

Acid Jazz

Sly re-branding of **Jazz funk** to take advantage of the

Acid House boom in 1988. As in: 'Jus' Reach' by Galliano.

Acid Rock

From 1966 onwards, the blues played on drugs. As in: 'In-A-Gadda-Da-Vida' by Iron Butterfly.

Alternative

Originally indicated any act from outside the radio/retail mainstream. Became meaningless with the success of U2, REM, Nirvana, etc. Now hangs around as a token of one's identification with the outsiders. As in: 'Loser' by Beck.

Alt.country

Country-ish sound made by pasty-faced guitar bands who pose for photographs in trailer parks. As in: 'Sweet Jane' by the Cowboy Junkies.

Alt.rock

The alternative to **Alternative**, embracing every harder-to-get-into variant on the white boys with guitar template. As in: everything from Tortoise to Tool.

Ambient

Ethereal electronic background music. As in: 'The Pearl' by Brian Eno and Harold Budd.

Ambient house

Version of house music without the drums. Quite

druggy. As in: 'A Huge Ever-Growing Pulsating Brain That Rules from the Centre of the Ultraworld' by The Orb.

Americana

Country music that doesn't do big numbers. As in: 'Car Wheels on a Gravel Road' by Lucinda Williams.

AOR

Adult Oriented Rock. As in: Seal.

Arena Rock

Heavy metal with gristle removed. As in: 'You Ain't Seen Nothing Yet' by Bachman Turner Overdrive.

B

Baggy

Car thief music, the sound of summer 1991. As in: 'Step On' by Happy Mondays.

Beat Music

American rock and roll songs played by tinny English guitar bands circa 1963. As in: 'Needles And Pins' by The Searchers.

Big Beat

Loud, bright, very layered, chart-friendly dance music favoured by *FHM* readers in the late 1990s. As in: 'The Rockefella Skank' by Fatboy Slim.

Blue-Eyed Soul

Soul music sung by white men. As in: 'She's Gone' by Hall And Oates.

Blues

Elementary, twelve-bar guitar-based music invented by economically disadvantaged African-Americans (like most of the stuff here). As in: 'Mannish Boy' by Muddy Waters.

Breakbeat

Any loop of sampled drums, as used in hip hop and dance music. Also generic catch-all for less lairy end of **Jungle** and **Big Beat**. As in: 'Smack My Bitch Up' by The Prodigy.

Brill Building

Yearning teenage pop from era before The Beatles. Named after offices where publishers were based. As in: 'It Might As Well Rain Until September' by Carole King.

Britpop

1990s phenomenon in which Oasis and Blur self-consciously emulated The Beatles and The Kinks and London swung (allegedly). As in: 'Country House' by Blur.

Bubblegum

Bright, light, factory-made pop music of the late

1960s aimed at pre-teens and often based on playground chants. As in: 'Yummy Yummy Yummy (I've Got Love In My Tummy)' by Ohio Express.

C

Cajun

The accordion-based formal dance music of southwest Louisiana. As in: 'Step It Fast' by Nathan Abshire.

Chill

As Neil Tennant has it, 'music for listening to in the bath'. As in: 'In The Bath' by Lemon Jelly.

Complaint rock

Alt.rock offshoot centring on injustices perpetrated against teens by adults, government, religion, etc. Identified in the film *Clueless*. As in: 'Jagged Little Pill' by Alanis Morissette.

Country

The folk-song-derived popular music of the rural whites of America. As in: 'The Fighting Side of Me' by Merle Haggard.

Country-rock

Rock bands playing country songs in truck drivers' clothes. As in: 'Six Days on the Road' by The Flying Burrito Brothers.

D

Dancehall

Rapped reggae over drum machines. Rude, usually. As in: 'Boombastic' by Shaggy.

Death Metal

Heavy metal about death. As in: 'Greed Killing' by Napalm Death.

Delta Blues

Blues from the delta of the Mississippi river. As in: 'Crossroads' by Robert Johnson.

Disco

Records made to be danced to in establishments solely dedicated to dancing. As in: 'Disco Inferno' by The Trammps.

Doowop

Street-corner vocal quartets with voice imitating bass (hence the name). As in: 'Get A Job' by The Silhouettes.

Drill'n'Bass

Borderline unlistenable, fast variant on **Drum'n'Bass** from UK avant-garde/mickey-taking producers. As in: 'Hard Normal Daddy' by Squarepusher.

Drum'n'Bass

(1) (1970s) Minimalist reggae – does what it says on the tin. See also **Dub**. As in: 'King Tubby Meets the

Rockers Uptown' by Augustus Pablo. (2) (1990s) Reggae and R&B **Breakbeats** accelerated, often rapped over. Aka **Jungle**. As in: 'Inner City Life' by Goldie.

E

Electro

Early hip hop, concerned with partying and pretending to be a robot/from space rather than money/women/shooting people. As in: 'Planet Rock' by Afrika Bambaataa and Soul Sonic Force.

Electroclash

Return of **Electro** in early twenty-first century in new-found fashion/gay finery. As in: 'Emerge' by Fischerspooner.

Electronica

What Americans call dance music. As in: everything from Air to Meat Beat Manifesto.

Emo

When hardcore bands go lyrical. As in: 'Margin Walker' by Fugazi.

Europop

Shrill crowd-pleasers by cross-channel artistes in the universal Esperanto of gobbledegook. Little appeal to the over-fives. As in: 'Blue (Da Ba Dee)' by Eiffel '65.

F

Filtered Disco

Take a chunk of an old **Disco** record, mess it about in the studio, presto. The French were especially good at this. As in: 'Music Sounds Better With You' by Stardust.

Folk Rock

Started off meaning folk-songs played on electric guitars. Ended up denoting songs composed on acoustic guitar and performed by an electric band. As in: 'Mr Tambourine Man' by The Byrds.

Fratrock

Dumb party music for guys in togas to dance to without spilling their beer. As in: 'Woolly Bully' by Sam the Sham and The Pharaohs.

Funk

Originally described the smell of sex, it was used in the 1970s to describe the sound of black music moving away from songs towards grooves. As in: 'One Nation Under a Groove' by Funkadelic.

Fusion

See **Jazz Funk**.

G

Gabba
Punishingly fast Dutch variant on **Techno**, pronounced 'habber'. As in: 'Poing' by Rotterdam Termination Source.

Gangsta Rap
Rapping about being a gangster. As in: 'Nothing But A G Thang' by Doctor Dre.

Garage
(1) Bog-standard, DIY American pre-punk from the late 1960s. As in: '96 Tears' by ? And The Mysterians. (2) Loverman-ish, song-based New Jersey variant on **House**. Aka **Deep House**. As in: 'That's The Way Love Is' by Ten City. (3) UK Garage: House tracks plus stuttering, hip hop drum machines and reggae MCing. Aka **Speed Garage** (pronounced 'garridge'). As in: '21 Seconds' by So Solid Crew.

G-Funk
Mid-1990s hip hop discovers the ancient grooves of **P-Funk**. As in: 'Regulate' by Warren G.

Glam-Rock
Bizarre, essentially British school of early 1970s pop in which groups adopted spangly clothing that belied the Watney's Red Barrel flavour of their sound. As in: 'Blockbuster' by The Sweet.

Gospel

Sacred music of the American South presented as entertainment. As in: 'Jesus Hits Like An Atom Bomb' by The Pilgrim Travellers.

Goth Rock

The doomy sound you make after overdoing the hair products and painting your light bulb red. As in: 'Wasteland' by The Mission.

Grunge

Amalgam of hard rock sound and punk attitude developed by a generation of Americans who'd spent time with the educational psychiatrist. As in: 'Smells Like Teen Spirit' by Nirvana.

H

Hair bands

Arena Rock bands dressing up for MTV in the 1980s. As in: 'Bad Medicine' by Bon Jovi.

Handbag

Light, disco-inflected variant on **House**, beloved of hen parties and transvestites, named after the thing you dance around. As in: 'One Night In Heaven' by M People.

Hardcore

(1) Strictly moralistic 1980s US punk. As in: 'Don't

Want To Know If You Are Lonely' by Hüsker Dü.
(2) Abrasive, fundamentalist early '90s faction of
Rave. As in: 'Activ 8' by Altern 8.

Hard Rock

Loud, guitar-driven rock with shouty vocals from
men in hipster trousers. As in: 'Walk This Way' by
Aerosmith.

Heavy Metal

Loud, repetitive, highly formal, guitar-based music
aimed at boys (who will be boys). As in: 'You Shook
Me All Night Long' by AC/DC.

Hi-Nrg

Gay-friendly dance music that emerged in the early
1980s. Emphasis on the beat and female lead vocal.
As in: 'Searchin' by Hazell Dean.

Hip Hop

Catch-all term for the music and culture that began
with the rap revolution of the 1980s and wound up
being as huge, pervasive and various as rock. As in:
'It Takes Two' by Rob Base.

House

Largely mechanised dance music that emerged from
the warehouse parties of Chicago to take over the
world in the mid-1980s. Characterised by very long
tracks. As in: 'Move Your Body' by Marshall Jefferson.

I

Indie
Originally indicated the independent status of one's record label. Now that these labels are owned by majors it means anyone *NME* enthuses about. As in: 'Jacqueline' by Franz Ferdinand.

J

Jazz
Largely instrumental African-American music with emphasis on improvisation around familiar themes. As in: 'Beale Street Blues' by Louis Armstrong.

Jazz Funk
Jazz musicians wear kaftans and discover the power of the groove in the 1970s. As in: 'Headhunters' by Herbie Hancock.

Jazz-Rock
Hybrid created by the addition of horn sections to rock bands in the late 1960s. As in: 'Spinning Wheel' by Blood, Sweat & Tears.

Jungle
See **Drum'n'Bass**.

K

Kraut Rock

Mechanised electronic music pioneered by Germans in the early 1970s. As in: 'Autobahn' by Kraftwerk.

L

Latte

Young people who can Really Play produce jazz-inflected easy listening aimed at Radio Two audience. As in: 'Come Away With Me' by Norah Jones.

Lounge

Schlock from the 1960s and '70s which is weird enough to sound hip. As in: 'Harlem Nocturne' by Esquivel.

Lovers' Rock

Soupy reggae. As in: 'All I Have Is Love' by Gregory Isaacs.

M

Math Rock

Rock for nerds. As in: 'At Action Park' by Shellac.

Mersey Beat

Liverpudlian variant of **Beat Music**. As in: 'You're No Good' by Swinging Blue Jeans.

New age

Instrumental music *sans* tunes, the better to accompany meditation. Sometimes mockingly pronounced to rhyme with 'sewage'. As in: 'Tubular Bells' by Mike Oldfield.

New Jack Swing

The reaction of mainstream black pop to the arrival of hip hop was to put a drum machine and a bit of rap on every record. As in: 'Every Little Step' by Bobby Brown.

New Romantic

You can get away with a lot with a tea-towel and some eyeliner. As in: 'Fade To Grey' by Visage.

New Wave

Weasel term used to sell punk to the mainstream and the mainstream to punk. As in: 'Oliver's Army' by Elvis Costello.

No Wave

Really difficult jazz plus really difficult rock. Bet you're sorry you missed that. As in: 'Contort Yourself' by James White And The Blacks.

Northern Soul

1960s soul played for frantic, amphetamine-fuelled dancing in clubs in the north of England. As in:

'Open the Door to Your Heart' by Darrell Banks.

NWOBHM

New Wave Of British Heavy Metal (from the early 1980s). As in: 'Run To The Hills' by Iron Maiden.

O

Oi

Politically dubious, short-lived celebration of yobbery championed by Garry Bushell in the early 1980s. The musical articulation of the Millwall chant 'No one likes us/we don't care'. As in: 'Oi! Oi! Oi!' by The Cockney Rejects.

P

P-Funk

R&B and soul plus an enormous amount of drugs. As in: 'Give Up the Funk (Tear The Roof Off The Sucker)' by Parliament.

Pop

Popular music. Employed condescendingly by 'rock' supremacists. As in: anything from Frank Sinatra to The White Stripes.

Post-Rock

Prog rock with crippling shyness. As in: 'Taut And Tame' by Tortoise.

Progressive
Variant of **Hard Rock** in which each member gets chance to demonstrate their mastery of difficult bits. Big on space and pixies. As in: 'Close to the Edge' by Yes.

Progressive House
Snooty term coined to differentiate 'grown-up', metropolitan dance music from the cheesy fare preferred by peasant ravers. As in: 'Song Of Life' by Leftfield.

Psychedelia
Music that sounds as if it were imagined and played on mind-expanding chemicals. As in: 'Strawberry Fields Forever' by The Beatles.

Psychobilly
Horror-show rockabilly; 90 per cent about haircut. As in: 'The Crusher' by The Cramps.

Pub Rock
Guitar music played in London pubs in the mid-1970s back-to-the-roots move. As in: 'Surrender to the Rhythm' by Brinsley Schwarz.

Punk
Rock and roll returned to its three-chord roots in the late 1970s but with unsentimental attitude, bags of speed and mistreated hair. As in: 'White Riot' by The Clash.

Post-Punk

Artier bunch emboldened by punk. As in: 'Love Will Tear Us Apart' by Joy Division.

Powerpop

1960s beat music revived by '70s guys in skinny ties with jacket sleeves rolled back. As in: 'My Sharona' by The Knack.

Q

Quiet Storm

Boudoir soul aimed at older, more affluent black audiences, named after Smokey Robinson album. As in: 'Sexual Healing' by Marvin Gaye.

R

Ragga

Digital reggae. As in: 'Here Comes the Hot Stepper' by Ini Kamoze.

Rare Groove

Old 1970s soul records given new lease of life in the late 1980s. As in: 'Cross The Tracks' by Maceo & The Macks.

Rave

Cheapest and least pretentious variant of 1990s dance music. Heavy on the airhorns. As in: 'Everybody's

Free' by Rozalla.

Reggae

The indigenous pop music of the island of Jamaica. New Orleans rhythm and blues as re-arranged through a skull full of marijuana. As in: 'Stir It Up' by Bob Marley and the Wailers.

R&B

The dominant sound of today's pop. As in: 'Crazy In Love' by Beyoncé.

Rhythm and Blues

The popular music that sprang from the blues in the 1960s. As in: 'What'd I Say' by Ray Charles.

Rock

Used by radio to denote 'white'.

Rock and Roll

Black slang for the sex act applied by Alan Freed to 1950s rhythm and blues aimed at a white audience. As in: 'Summertime Blues' by Eddie Cochran.

Rockabilly

Hybrid of rock and hillbilly played by hoodlum cats from shallow end of the Kentucky gene pool. As in: 'Dixie Fried' by Carl Perkins.

S

Salsa

The dance music of Central America. Spanish for 'sauce'. As in: 'Acid' by Ray Barretto.

Soft Rock

Music for eight-track cartridges. As in: 'Guitar Man' by Bread.

Shoegazing

1990s variant of British indie rock in which guitar bands went in for high-volume washes of sound while hiding behind their fringes and inspecting their laces. As in: 'Vapour Trail' by Ride.

Ska

Jamaican jazz musicians making simple, danceable pop music in the 1960s. As in: 'Train to Skaville' by The Ethiopians.

Skatepunk

Hardcore punk favoured by skaters. As in: 'You Can't Bring Me Down' by Suicidal Tendencies.

Skiffle

Low-budget British take on the jug band sound popular in the 1950s. Involved those extinct household items the washboard and the tea chest. As in: 'Rock Island Line' by Lonnie Donegan.

Soul

Umbrella for vast range of black American music, generally characterised by deeply felt vocal style with roots in church music. However, soul is as much a property as a genre. As in: 'When a Man Loves a Woman' by Percy Sledge.

Southern Rock

Countrified, lyrical strain of hard rock played by longhairs from below Mason-Dixon line. What would have happened if The Grateful Dead had rehearsed and could sing. As in: 'Whipping Post' by The Allman Brothers Band.

Space Rock

Bare-breasted Earth Mother fronting nose-bleed metal band. As in: 'Silver Machine' by Hawkwind.

Speed Garage

See **Garage, UK**.

Surf Music

Largely instrumental guitar music from the early 1960s. At its best outdoors. As in: 'Let's Go Trippin'' by Dick Dale

Swamp-Rock

Bassy, sensual variant from Louisiana. Big on bull-frogs and backwoods preachers. As in: 'Polk Salad Annie' by Tony Joe White.

T

Techno
Detroit-born music described as 'Kraftwerk trapped in an elevator with George Clinton'. As in: 'Strings Of Life' by Rythim Is Rythim.

Tex-Mex
Accordion-based, Hispanic-influenced music of the Texas–Mexican border. As in: 'Wasted Days And Wasted Nights' by Freddie Fender.

Thrash Metal
Where punk met heavy metal. Black! Black! Black! As in: 'Fade To Black' by Metallica.

Trance
European development of house music with the emphasis on endless repetition. European development of house music with the emphasis on endless repetition. European development of house music with the emphasis on endless repetition. As in: 'Café Del Mar' by Energy 52.

Trip Hop
Downbeat, arty variant of hip hop. As in: 'Glory Box' by Portishead.

Turbo-folk
Virulently nationalist Serbian folk songs with pounding dance beat. As in: 'Balkan Boj' by Rambo Amadeus.

Turntablism

Impressing people by playing your funky old records in clever ways. As in: 'Endtroducing' by DJ Shadow.

U

Underground

Useful prefix for any music that doesn't sell an awful lot.

Urban

Used by radio to denote 'black'.

W

West Coast

The highly polished, summery sound of Los Angeles studio productions. As in: 'The Boys of Summer' by Don Henley.

Western Swing

Jazz played by cowboys. As in: 'Take Me Back to Tulsa' by Bob Wills and his Texas Playboys.

World Music

Anything not containing the word 'baby'.

ACKNOWLEDGEMENTS

This book came out of a series of features in *Word* magazine and wouldn't be what it is without the input of everyone there, particularly Mark Ellen, Paul Du Noyer, Andrew Harrison, Keith Drummond, Jude Rogers, Dan Reeves and Jerry Perkins. Thanks also to Spencer Leigh for the Sinatra story and John Naughton for Delia Smith's cake.

ILLUSTRATION CREDITS

Hoagy Carmichael. Photograph © Bettmann/Corbis
Walter Carlos. Photograph © Bettmann/Corbis
The Rolling Stones with Ian Stewart. Photograph ©
    Dezo Hoffmann/Rex Features
Rin Tin Tin. Photograph © Getty Images
The Graduate film poster. Photograph © Getty
    Images
2002 Oscars Rehearsal. Photograph © Getty Images
George Harrison and Patti Boyd. Photograph ©
    Getty Images
Eric Clapton and Patti Harrison. Photograph ©
    Getty Images